A Manual

of Intergroup Relations

A Manual
of Intergroup Relations

By JOHN P. DEAN and ALEX ROSEN

with the assistance of

ROBERT B. JOHNSON

Foreword by CHARLES S. JOHNSON
Introduction by EDWARD A. SUCHMAN and
ROBIN M. WILLIAMS, JR.
New Preface by
ALEX ROSEN and ROBERT B. JOHNSON

PHOENIX BOOKS

The University of Chicago Press

CHICAGO & LONDON

Library of Congress Catalog Card Number: 56-5141

THE UNIVERSITY OF CHICAGO PRESS, CHICAGO & LONDON
The University of Toronto Press, Toronto 5, Canada

*This edition is dedicated to the memory of
Professor* JOHN P. DEAN, *co-author of the book
and director of the research on which it is based,
and* DR. CHARLES S. JOHNSON,
former President of Fisk University.

Foreword

There has been developing over the past decade a new profession, within the broad context of the social sciences. It emerges out of the need in our time for skilful mediation of intergroup relations in our society. The requirement for such mediation has been present for a long time. There have been attempts, in nonspecialized but well-intentioned ways, to deal with the problems of intergroup tensions by a variety of individuals and organizations concerned with the common welfare. The difference is very much like that which exists in the social sciences between the charitable individual and the professionally trained social worker or practitioner.

Our American democratic society, with its myriad cultural and social backgrounds, in a period of deep and far-reaching change, faces a new urgency in intergroup relations within the democratic context of the society itself. The complex of social, economic, psychological, and cultural involvements of these relations is such as to require the best efforts and skills of the behavioral sciences in study and analysis. Over the years a considerable amount of knowledge has been accumulated, but until recently it has not been systematically organized for use in actual social situations.

There is no longer an indefinite period of time ahead for the leisurely attrition of personal attitudes in adjusting to the new imperatives of social relations. Social changes of a profoundly important character, involving the adjustment of widely diverse groups, are already under way. They are a result of forces stronger and wider than any that can be generated in a single community. The most intelligent action is to get acquainted with these forces and utilize them for the common good of our society. This is more than indiscriminate good will or humaneness, however vital these qualities might be for the spirit of the good society. In its technical phases this more systematic approach to group relations is an art and a profession. The profession is still in its infancy, but there is no doubt about the need for such professionally trained practitioners.

The present volume is a venture in the direction of making available for intergroup practitioners some of the tested observations of social scientists in direct application to social situations. The social scientists responsible for the observations and deductions, one a practitioner and one not, are sufficiently concerned about the usefulness of a body of knowledge and intelligent inference to the enlightened management of human relations to take this first exploratory step. They quite properly make no claim to finality of judgment in these matters, but their projections have a value far superior to the random activities often associated with intergroup management.

The experience upon which these observations and projections are based is, without question, the most intensive series of controlled studies of intergroup behavior in recent times in which competent social scientists have been engaged. It is fortunate that the results, so far tentatively accepted, are available for test and application in the present racial situation involving readjustment of group attitudes and practices over a wide area of American life. Without some guides to action, there can be hopeless confusion in programs and plans, or still worse, paralysis of effort. Whatever the value of this volume to practitioners and organizations in the various social settings of the nation, it is certain that the ends sought in the projections are consistent with the highest ends of our democratic society and government.

CHARLES S. JOHNSON
President, Fisk University

Preface

Frederick the Great of Prussia once said, "An experience is of little value unless one reflects upon it." The authors of this book have followed this dictum in their practice and in their research efforts. This book is based upon such research. It was a type of research somewhat unusual not only in its execution but also in the characteristics of the researchers themselves. For the authors in their professional careers have been not only academicians but practitioners as well. A decade ago, when the original research on which this book is based was done, the authors, one a social scientist, the other a social work practitioner, were "doubly" engaged; we were involved in purposive social action research and at the same time were self-consciously studying it.

We thought of ourselves as both participants and observers, as actors and critics, and as being on-stage and off-stage at one and the same time. It is this duality that characterizes this book. It is a duality of action and thought, of theory and practice, of doing and thinking. The authors not only wrote this book; we actually participated in the experiences and experiments which are described in various places in the text.

Thus we hoped to produce another duality—a book which had not only sensitivity to the immediacy of the practitioners' experiences but also a detached objectivity which would give to the experience a deeper perspective and thus facilitate greater understanding.

Students in schools of social work and other young professionals find this concept of "nearness and distance" one of the most fruitful, and yet one of the most difficult, to master. As Wilensky and Lebeaux put it in their book *Industrial Society and Social Welfare:*

All human relations blend social nearness and distance; and the dilemma of involvement and detachment is not new to our time. For social work (as well as for psychotherapy) the term "objectivity" takes its place beside "rapport" as a characterization of the client-professional relationship. Together they comprise in Mannheim's words a "strange combination of intimacy and objectivity, nearness and distance, attraction and repulsion, friendship and estrangement," a combination which the professional in training (especially one who works in an intimate field like social work) finds difficult to comprehend and incorporate into his habit patterns. When it is grasped and "learned in the muscles," then the novitiate has developed the essence of the "professional self."

Representing two different professional disciplines—sociology and social work—the authors have had the self-conscious professional orientation just described. Such an orientation is in counterdistinction to the approaches based on rough rules of thumb, intuition, or the mere application of good will. "Love is truly not enough." For when an activity or occupation aspires to a "professional mandate" (meaning society sanctions and values it as effective) a fundamental prerequisite is a body of scholarly knowledge containing tested formulations which describe the relationship between "functional expertise" and the set of intended goals which these measures are aimed at achieving. This is what we tried to accomplish in our book.

Thus the reader of this edition will note that the book contains a series of numbered propositions. These represent the authors' conclusions in succinct, declarative form. They are not intended, however, to be utilized as simplistic "how-to-do-it" prescriptions. Social change is too complex to be reduced to formulas or "cookbook recipes." Rather these propositions are a series of perspectives, implications, and generalizations intended as guides to insight, to understanding, and, finally, for action. The reader, applying these propositions, will need to be sensitive to the dissimilarities, as well as similarities, of certain situations; he will need an awareness of the need to weight, test, and modify his concepts with new knowledge and new circumstances.

The reader of this edition may now well ask, "Well and good—it's now several years since the first of three printings was published. How has it stood the test of time? How has it measured against the complexity and rapidity of change in our social order?" A comprehensive answer would be another study. However, in a limited way, some major indications can be identified for the guidance of the reader.

The authors have tried to assess this experience with the help of a number of officers of national organizations which have utilized the book in various ways, such as institutes and training seminars. What comes through first is the usefulness to the practitioners of the material in the book dealing with the *1.* strategy directed toward the change of behavior rather than change in personality or attitudes (see chap. v and propositions 6, 7, 8, 9). It is social change, behavioral change, not personality change, toward which this book is directed. We argue that much behavioral change is possible despite the "level of prejudice in a particular individual." The counterargument is still current that "we cannot legislate morality before we change mens' hearts." Laws, however, can change behavior and social practices, and that is our major concern. If housing, employment, and education, for instance, can be truly integrated, we will be on our way to achieving a more equitable social order. The point made in the book is precisely this—that men's behavior has wide latitude, despite what is in their "hearts."

Practitioners have also found helpful the material on "the process of maturation" (see chap. iv). Of particular interest *2,* was the description in this chapter of the personal experiences of a young white social worker who had her first experiences in a youth program with Negro members. In a very frank, honest statement, she describes her "embarrassments, discomforts, soul-searching, and thoughtful reflections," as she matured in experience and understanding. This description of a young person's inner feelings seems to have struck a responsive chord among many other young people (both agency members and young professional workers) who were experiencing similar feelings and attitudes as they struggled for greater self-insight and maturity. This chapter also contains a summary of the types of knowledge, attitudes, and skills which our data suggested distinguished the effective practitioner from the ineffective practitioner. Since a profession is based upon identified and communicable "knowledge, attitudes, and skill," this section is of particular value to professional staff.

Another major characteristic of the approach in this book is the distinction made between desegregation and integration (see chap. vi). The authors arrived independently at this differentiation, and it represented to them one of the major findings of the book (see chaps. vi, vii, and ix). We viewed desegregation as a goal achievable rather quickly as schools and social agencies become more diversified in membership and participation. Integration, on the other hand, we viewed as a long-range *process* of education—a process of unlearning prejudices and of establishing new democratic values through interaction in a nonsegregated environment.

The material in the text dealing with problems of communication among people different in race, color, and creed, and especially the "language of prejudice" (see chaps. ii and iii), represents some of the first generalizations based on social science data in this most subtle area of human interaction. Certainly, it has been more than substantiated that minority participation is essential in any effective intergroup relations program. The past decade's experiences have, however, carried this concept much further. For today, as spelled out more specifically below in this Preface, there has developed the new Negro, more self-reliant, more courageous, who even in the South is changing the patterns of race relations and of the social structure by such techniques as "sit-ins" and nonviolent community action.

We turn now to an evaluation of the status of intergroup relations in the 1960's against the background of the propositions presented in our *Manual* a decade ago. We would be remiss if we did not acknowledge the impact of recent changes in civil rights. These recent events have strengthened our belief in the propositions stated in the original *Manual*. However, there are areas where we have altered the salience of our original belief about the more significant factors affecting social change in intergroup relations. We wish to comment upon some of those changes in our emphasis.

The Past Ten Years

Much has happened in intergroup relations since the findings were recorded ten years ago. The momentous Supreme Court decision of 1954, which outlawed segregation in public education, had a massive impact upon all Americans. In addition, the rapid and still accelerated emergence of the African and other nonwhite nations in world affairs has given American minorities a heightened sense of self-confidence and an awareness that movement and social change are possible.

We believe that an even more significant cluster of historical factors have affected the status of American intergroup relations today. For example, as Negro Americans approached the hundredth anniversary of Lincoln's signing of the Emancipation Proclamation, it was evident that there was a mounting impatience with the slow process of racial integration and with the leisurely or reluctant manner with which southern white policy-makers were complying with the Supreme Court decision against public school segregation.

Thus there appeared to be an acceleration of the waves of action to achieve racial equality. Shortly after the 1954 Supreme Court decision, an NAACP membership campaign drive warned members that "if you want to be free by '63—you got to do more in '54." Then came a series of increasingly urgent actions in race relations: desegregation of schools in Louisville, Washington, Baltimore, and other border cities; the creative nonviolent bus boycott; the violence in Little Rock, Arkansas, and Clinton, Tennessee, which resulted in the summoning of federal troops.

And then what was fast becoming a massive social movement reached a new crest. On February 1, 1960, the *Southern School News*, a newspaper devoted to reporting changing events in southern race relations, reported that six years after the Supreme Court decision only 6 per cent of southern Negroes were attending racially desegregated schools. It became apparent that at this rate total desegregation of southern schools would not be accomplished for one hundred years. By sheer coincidence it was on that same date that four Negro students in Greensboro, North Carolina, entered a downtown variety store and, after making purchases, sat down at the lunch counter and requested service. The store's refusal to serve them, coupled with the urgency that many youths feel today, set off a chain reaction of spontaneous demonstrations, now known as "sit-ins." This protest touched almost every major community in the South and resulted in a massive social movement involving over 50,000 Negro students and resulting in arrests of at least 10,000 nonviolent but insistent student demonstrators.

Since that time we have witnessed a wave of similar "direct-action" demonstrations—the freedom rides, the stand-ins, kneel-ins, wade-ins, and now the Domestic Vote Core where Negro and white students are working full time in the Deep South in an effort to alter and reform political institutions through voter-education programs, particularly among rural Negro share-croppers.

The Intergroup Relations Community versus Direct Social Action

The philosophy and technique of this southern movement has spread to other parts of the country. Persons interested in civil rights—particularly the youths of all races—have unleashed a new set of social forces in numerous American communities. In some cases, these direct-action forces have challenged or ignored the traditional and established intergroup relations "community" and have caused it to re-examine its own techniques of establishing patterns of effective community action. It is for this reason that professional and lay persons have cast about for methods of procedure that might reconcile patterns of direct social action with patterns of established community organization in intergroup relations, to mold them into an efficient social force that will act with a maximum of effectiveness.

A Re-examination of Community Power Structure

Our experiences and observations in the past ten years have intensified our belief in the necessity of identifying and understanding that interlocking leadership system in American communities frequently referred to as "Community Power Structure." Events such as the southern bus boycotts, sit-ins, and freedom rides are examples of social protest movement which the established community power structure was powerless to stop.

These events have reminded us that the conventional conception of power structure must be expanded to include a wide variety of sources of community power, whether these sources stem from religious fervor, invocations of outside sanctions, minority bloc voting, programs of social reform, or other social movements. We have noted occasions where conventional power forces that once opposed social change in intergroup relations seem rapidly to accept the change, praise it, and sometimes actually take credit for it. We note that the "unthinkables" of yesterday are becoming the "taken-for-granteds" of today; the "unthinkables" of today may very well become the "taken-for-granteds" of tomorrow, with the established community power structure either gracefully or reluctantly accepting the change.

As an example, ten years ago it was well-nigh unthinkable that Negroes in the South might use the facilities of trains, busses, and other means of public transportation. Subsequent rulings against segregation in public transportation by the Supreme Court and by the Interstate Commerce Commission seemed to have had little effect on this pattern of segregation.

However, in 1961 civil rights forces unleashed a program of direct action now known as "freedom rides" in which many more of these southern transportation facilities were tested. This action touched off numerous arrests, beatings, and jailings of the freedom riders and led the Department of Justice to plead for a moratorium on freedom rides in order to prevent further injuries or possible deaths. Civil rights leaders, particularly the college students who had witnessed considerable success with the "sit-in" technique, insisted on continuing the freedom rides until the pattern of segregation in transportation was completely removed.

Despite the heightened number of arrests that followed, the United States Attorney-General was able to announce in 1963 that segregation in interstate transportation had ceased to exist in all cities but one. This is but one example among many where the power of protest within a minority community was strong enough to overcome the reluctance of community "gatekeepers" to change their pattern of behavior.

Direct Action and the Intergroup Relations Community

In many communities there has been a breakdown in interpersonal communication that should be noted. In the civil rights field there are now two different approaches which frequently come into conflict, and this may result in such a breakdown. One of the approaches is that of the traditional intergroup relations community guided by members of established agencies who have developed traditional ways of doing things. The new protest, sparked by the events in the South, is made up generally of people who are not organized in the same way and whose approach tends to be different. In fact, they value "underorganization" because they perceive organization as being sometimes a strait jacket to activity. This newer force is more likely to carry on direct action than to wait for the process of law. The older group feels that movements and demonstrations cannot affect such problems as those caused by urban renewal or automation. The new group answers that they have waited too long to see things *change*, that they want to *see it all changed*, and they want to see it all changed *now*. We feel that effective community organization needs to reconcile the sharp clash between these two forces.

Background Changes

As Whitney M. Young, Jr., executive director of the National Urban League, has pointed out, there has been an increasing awareness on the part of Negro and white citizens alike of the changing nature of the problem of race in our society. One of the most dramatic changes has been the continuing urbanization of the American Negro. It is estimated that, by 1975, 85 per cent of all Negro citizens will live in major urban centers, mainly in the North. Cities like Detroit, Chicago, and New York will be the rule rather than the exception. Because of the unemployment, housing discrimination, and other differential life conditions still characteristic of the Negro's situation, it can be anticipated that friction, frustration, and bitterness will prevail to a degree in these mass urban centers. This continued migration and urbanization is a major and critical factor to be noted in the next decade and will undoubtedly affect the status of race relations in our society.

In addition, it can be anticipated, unless there is massive governmental intervention on state and federal levels, that automation will make expendable large numbers of employees. A disproportionately high number of Negro workers, because they occupy the unskilled and semiskilled jobs, will be most affected.

The Negro community, it can also be anticipated for the next decade, will be affected by urban renewal, slum clearance, and superhighway construction. The "inner core" of many a major city has become educationally, culturally, and socially sub-standard, and it is to this region that the displaced Negro finds himself segregated, paradoxically enough, because of "progressive" city planning.

Conclusion

Our experience as colleagues, as observers of the intergroup relations scene, and as personal friends have strengthened our conviction about the fruitfulness of collaboration and exchange of ideas between social scientist and social worker. It is for this reason, among many others, that we have dedicated this book to two students of human behavior who had a vision of what good things might come out of this professional collaboration: John P. Dean and Charles J. Johnson.

In our recent intergroup relations experience we have been gratified by the opportunity to "carry a small spear in a big production." We are pleased to feel that in our small way we have been watching the production, playing a role, and helping to write the script. This book represents part of our script-writing effort.

ALEX ROSEN
ROBERT B. JOHNSON

March 1963

Introduction

For some years the world situation in intergroup relations has been changing, often accompanied by conflict and tension. Here in the United States the social changes set in motion by World War II led to great mobility among different groups of people, to community restlessness, and to fears of social tensions and riots. Mayors' committees and interracial commissions sprang up to handle the possible outbreak of violence.

Sometimes the anticipated tension did occur, but more frequently it did not. Negroes, Jews, and foreign-born were introduced into hundreds of jobs at which they had never before worked. New social contacts and friendships often grew naturally out of the widening opportunities for contact, and it was found that in many new settings nonsegregated patterns worked out perfectly well.

No one seemed to understand just what the crucial things were that made one situation explosive and another harmonious and acceptable. But research projects were begun, and little by little the administrators and practitioners began to accumulate experience that provided rough rules of thumb to guide intergroup practices.

Emerging from accumulated intergroup experience and from ongoing social science research are a few major principles that have implications for intergroup practices far beyond those usually found in much current literature on intergroup relations. The aim of the authors of this volume has been to set these major propositions in clear perspective and to discuss their implications for the many practitioners who are struggling every day to deal with intergroup relations in the communities where they are now working.

But first a word of qualification. A research group such as

the one conducting the Cornell studies in intergroup relations is occasionally asked to develop the implications of its research for specific real-life situations. The customary reply of a research group is to point out that they are social scientists and that specific applications of their findings must be made by individual practitioners in the light of (a) their values and immediate goal objectives and (b) the individual peculiarities of the local situation. This reply leaves it to the practitioner to dig out of scientific monographs the findings most relevant to his work and develop the implications himself.

We feel, however, that, in the interest of bringing social science and social practice together, the social scientist should collaborate more with the practitioner in developing the practical implications of research work. At the risk of venturing beyond the boundaries of established scientific knowledge, then, the authors have evolved some tentative propositions about practices in intergroup relations. Although these propositions are the outgrowth of five years of research and of field investigations into hundreds of practical problems, they do not represent direct deductions from the scientific data. Instead, they represent the informed opinions of two collaborators, a social scientist and a practitioner, who have been working intensively in the field of intergroup relations. But as such they are the consensus of their reflection and judgment.

Naturally, propositions of this sort will have to be modified in the light of newly accumulating research evidence and the growing experience of practitioners. But, because of the urgency of the problem, it seems wise to set down our best current understanding of good intergroup practices "even before all the evidence is in." Besides, social scientists and practitioners alike know that the evidence is never all in. By setting their thoughts on paper, even in tentative form, the authors aim to provide a working manual that can be checked against the experiences of other practitioners and scientists and modified to represent more closely the accumulated wisdom of the field.

Most of the discussion has direct meaning for practitioners in organizations where different ethnic groups are involved—schools, housing authorities, recreational centers, group-work agencies, department stores, government agencies, factories, or even social and religious organizations. To be as concrete as possible, the authors have directed themselves to a particular group of practitioners, the group workers in settlement houses, Y's, and recreational centers. Most of the illustrations are chosen from this field. But the principles involved apply to intergroup practices in the other organizations, too. The recent Supreme Court decision forbidding segregation of the races in public schools throughout the land adds a new significance to any attempt to formulate the principles of good intergroup practice. The importance of the pages that follow for school administrators faced with desegregation is quite clear.

Group-work agencies, however, were chosen as the specific area of application for several reasons:

1. One of the authors is a social worker with training and experience in the field of group work. This background is invaluable in aiding the authors to develop the implications of social science findings for a concrete area of practice with which they are familiar. In some ways this is the major advantage of collaboration of this sort between practitioner and social scientist.

2. Social work provides ample case incidents and illustrations that make specific and meaningful the emerging "principles" of intergroup relations.

3. But, above and beyond these practical reasons for selecting social work as the area of collaboration between intergroup relations social science and intergroup relations practice, there are important substantive reasons. Youth and the teen-age years, when the individual is widening his horizons beyond neighborhood and home and beginning to loosen his bonds of dependence on the family, are times when significant personal growth through group experience is possible. The intergroup

values and sentiments laid down during this crucial period may set the main framework for the intergroup relations creed which the individual will carry with him for the rest of his life. The settlement house or recreation center offers an unusual laboratory for seeking the principles of intergroup relations. Thus intergroup relations represent an area of direct concern to group workers. Since group work aims to promote individual personality growth by modifying and making use of the *group* experiences of individuals, these new experiences in *inter*group relations offer important opportunities for personal growth.

Now a word or two about the origins of this project, the authors, and their methodology. For the last six years, under grants from the Rockefeller Foundation, the Cornell Social Science Research Center has been studying intergroup relations in a number of communities, especially ongoing action programs in intergroup relations. This program of study is oriented toward theory; the aim is to understand the processes of social change and the reasons why such changes occur. Action techniques are being appraised primarily for the scientific leads they give to these processes of change. The researchers recognized that the action interests of the research offered an unusual opportunity for practitioners to benefit substantially from this large-scale research, if the findings of social science could be converted into a form meaningful to the practitioner.

Russell Sage Foundation supported a trained professional worker in community organization to collaborate with the Cornell research team. His task was to work with them to codify the techniques of effective community action directed toward better intergroup relations. For a period of several years they have worked together to produce a handbook that would specify in useful form some of the principles and procedures of effective action in this field. This manual is based upon the large amount of research already completed in the field of intergroup relations.

The work has been under the supervision and guidance of the Cornell study's present staff, consisting of Robin M. Williams (director) and Edward A. Suchman (associate director). John P. Dean (field director) has had primary responsibility for the writing of the handbook.

The community organization worker for the task, Alex Rosen, is a person with appropriate qualifications: personal experience in intergroup relations work, experience in community organization work, training and experience in interviewing skills, and orientation in the field research techniques used by the Cornell research group in its community studies.

John P. Dean, the social scientist in the collaboration, was the field director of the Cornell studies in intergroup relations. He has been active in intergroup relations research for the last six years and is an active member of the National Association of Intergroup Relations Officials.

In addition to participating in the Cornell community studies, in which the staff did a thorough four-year study of one upstate New York community and briefer field studies of about twenty other communities, several special tasks were undertaken for this project: (1) the authors participated actively in the creation and ongoing activities of a mayor's committee on human relations; (2) they helped in the organization and conduct of five workshops in intergroup relations for social work practitioners; and (3) they accumulated a modest amount of quantitative data on intergroup practices in the group-work field. With the help of the national offices of two group-work organizations that have local affiliates throughout the country, the authors sent mail questionnaires to the local directors of a great many group-work agencies. The questionnaires of the four hundred or so directors who replied represent the accumulated wisdom and practices of thousands of man-hours of group-work experience in intergroup relations. From time to time throughout the book the authors have introduced the findings of this study.

Introduction

The handbook that has resulted from this collaboration is not, of course, anything like the final word in intergroup action techniques. It is hoped that it will be of practical value to professionals in the field. But an important part of the long-range task of formulating principles of sound social practice in the field of intergroup relations will be the continued testing and revising of the ideas presented here in the light of practitioners' experience throughout the country.

The fruitfulness of the collaboration between social scientist and practitioner on this task confirms our basic belief that social science findings have important practical implications for concrete fields of social practice.

EDWARD A. SUCHMAN
ROBIN M. WILLIAMS, JR.

Table of Contents

CHAPTER 1

Folklore and Sound Practice

Today thousands of administrators, executives, and professional workers are handling programs that directly involve intergroup relations. Yet there are few established principles of "good" intergroup practice. As things now stand, science and sound practice are disconcertingly mixed with myth and folklore. Administrators find it difficult to locate reliable guideposts amid a bewildering array of facts, opinions, and half-truths. Each works in his own way according to individual procedures and isolated judgments based on personal experience, preconceived notions, or vested organizational interests.

Many currently circulating beliefs appear to give almost diametrically opposed counsel on the causes and cures of intergroup problems. Here, for example, are five paired pieces of contradictory advice:

Bring people of different groups together and forget about race, and their prejudices will wither away.	*OR*	You can't just mix prejudiced people together; unless they are carefully prepared, you'll have tension and conflict.
You can't legislate away intergroup tensions; forcing the issue by laws will just antagonize people and cause delays.	*OR*	Fair employment practice laws have made hundreds of firms hire Negroes they would not otherwise have hired; we need strong mandatory laws.
Prejudiced people are emotionally sick; they can't be cured without therapy that goes to the root of their trouble.	*OR*	Most prejudice is pretty superficial; effective education will dispel most of the misconceptions people hold about minorities.

If you want to integrate Negroes into your organization, just do it quietly and inconspicuously, without telling anyone about it.	OR	The only sensible way to integrate Negroes into your organization is to sound out the members to see if they are ready for it.
We have to reach the rank and file by a more widespread use of radio, television, newspapers, and the like.	OR	Propaganda on race relations is not worth the money spent on it; we need education that will catch the individual when he is young and teachable.

Actually, experience and research indicate that all these statements contain some measure of truth, but that, as given, all are misleading. At the present stage of our knowledge, we cannot clearly tell which are sound principles of intergroup practice and which are merely unfounded or misleading opinions. Yet the purpose of this book is to do just that. We feel that the intergroup experience of the last twenty years and the growing body of intergroup research point rather clearly to a few major propositions that have enormous implications for social change in intergroup relations. We will try (*a*) to formulate these propositions as succinctly as possible (at some risk of oversimplifying) and (*b*) to draw from them what we believe are the major implications for intergroup relations practice.

It is obvious that we must judge these practices quite differently from one setting to another. Even the most casual observer is aware of wide variations in customs and sentiment from one region of the country to another, from one community to another, and even from one organization to another in the same community, despite the general acceptance of the American Creed.[1] In one setting, a practitioner in intergroup

1. Throughout this book reference is made to the "American Creed"—the body of ideals on which American society is based. Perhaps the best definition of the American Creed was given by Ralph Bunche: "Every man in the street, white, black, red or yellow, knows that this is 'the land of the free,' the 'land of opportunity,' the 'cradle of liberty,' the 'home of

relations can accomplish things that would be impossible in another. Despite these wide variations, we believe general criteria for evaluating "good intergroup relations practices" can be set up.

In our field research we have found it helpful to evaluate the status of intergroup relations practices by the following criteria:

1. Is genuine two-way communication taking place between the majority and minority groups, especially between the leaders?

2. Is the minority participating effectively in the formulation of policy and program in organizations that have different ethnic groups as members or staff?

3. Are the staffs of mixed organizations trained and experienced in intergroup relations?

4. Have those activities been desegregated that can reasonably be expected to be carried on jointly by different groups?

5. Are integrated activities being used to broaden the individual's understanding of other groups and to reinforce a personal creed devoted to democratic intergroup practices?

6. Are intergroup action organizations working for realistic objectives?

7. Is intergroup action work effectively organized, and has it involved key influential leaders in community life?

---

democracy,' that the American flag symbolizes the 'equality of all men' and guarantees to us all 'the protection of life, liberty and property,' freedom of speech, freedom of religion and racial tolerance" (quoted by Gunnar Myrdal in *An American Dilemma* [New York: Harper & Bros., 1944], p. 4). Myrdal goes on to say: "These ideals of the essential dignity of the individual human being, of the fundamental equality of all men, and of certain inalienable rights to freedom, justice, and a fair opportunity represent to the American people the essential meaning of the nation's early struggle for independence. In the clarity and intellectual boldness of the Enlightenment period these tenets were written into the Declaration of Independence, the Preamble of the Constitution, the Bill of Rights, and into the constitutions of the several states. The ideals of the American Creed have thus become the highest law of the land. The Supreme Court pays its reverence to these general principles when it declares what is constitutional and what is not" (*ibid.*, p. 5).

8. Are effective strategies being used by action organizations in negotiating for intergroup change?

9. Are practitioners in intergroup relations continuing to grow professionally in their understanding of intergroup relations?

One chapter is devoted to each of these criteria. The authors attempt to state a numbered series of "propositions." This not only helps us to be brief but also provides an opportunity for stating a particular finding in a concise, pithy way. There are, however, two disadvantages to this method: (a) the various propositions are not uniform—they are at different levels of abstraction, ranging from descriptions of social phenomena to correlations between different variables in social organization; (b) the various propositions are not organized into any conceptual framework forming a logical system. Rather, they are discrete assertions based upon research data. No attempt has been made to state every finding in propositional form, and the alert reader may draw for himself certain additional generalizations based upon the material presented.

PART I

Improving Intergroup Relations in Your Organization

CHAPTER 2

Problems of Communication[1]

If you are the director of an institution or organization that has activities in which different ethnic groups participate, you probably have on your staff or board some individuals (either from the majority group or from some minority) who have little experience in intergroup relations. Maybe these individuals have privately expressed their prejudices to you. Maybe their inexperience has been revealed to you through some blunder they have made in a mixed situation. In any case, you have an inkling of the person's naïveté, hesitate to draw this person into the intergroup relations program, and may even want to protect the person against situations that might cause embarrassment and discomfort. So you permit, perhaps even encourage, these inexperienced persons to minimize their contacts with the out-group and remain insulated until a later time when you think they may have arrived at a more appropriate democratic set of attitudes and opinions.

This course of action runs contrary to what our data suggest is a cardinal principle of intergroup relations:

PROPOSITION 1: *Sustained interaction between majority and minority is essential if the lines of communication and understanding necessary for an effective intergroup relations program are to be established.*

1. This chapter was written in collaboration with Robert B. Johnson, a member of the staff of the Cornell studies in intergroup relations from 1949 to 1954. Many of the ideas throughout this manual, but especially those of this and the following chapter, grew directly out of Johnson's studies of the Negro communities of several American cities. These studies are reported fully in "The Nature of the Minority Community" (unpublished Ph.D. dissertation, Cornell University, 1954).

Our research data show that for most people there is a consistently negative relationship between intergroup contact and intergroup prejudice. The more contact a person has with other groups, the lower is his level of general prejudice against them, as shown in Table 1. This result holds not only for majority-

TABLE 1

| | Amount of Contact* with Outgroup (Per Cent Low on Prejudice) | | |
	Low Contact	Medium Contact	High Contact
Majority-group adults:			
Elmira, N.Y.	45 (357)	....	62 (146)
Steubenville, Ohio	34 (180)	54 (80)	61 (28)
Savannah, Ga.	24 (45)	44 (251)	54 (58)
Majority-group youth:			
Elmira, N.Y.	23 (1,171)	34 (835)	47 (300)
Steubenville, Ohio, Protestant	31 (120)	45 (159)	52 (171)
Weirton, W.Va.	26 (306)	31 (118)	46 (51)
Minority-group adults:			
Elmira, N.Y., Negro	32 (73)	....	44 (77)
Steubenville, Ohio, Negro	51 (57)	59 (63)	85 (20)
Elmira, N.Y., Jewish	39 (59)	....	59 (91)
Steubenville, Ohio, Jewish	58 (29)	....	71 (38)
Minority-group youth:			
Elmira, N.Y., Negro	29 (45)	30 (23)	44 (32)
Elmira, N.Y., Jewish	27 (26)	....	54 (24)
Steubenville, Ohio, Negro	41 (97)	....	68 (50)
Weirton, W.Va., Negro	43 (31)	....	71 (65)
Steubenville, Ohio, Catholic	23 (176)	37 (191)	45 (144)

* Contact and prejudice indexes varied slightly from survey to survey. Numbers in parentheses refer to number of cases.

group prejudices but also for minority-group prejudices against the majority group. It holds for youth as well as for adults. In the Cornell University studies it is confirmed in fourteen different research surveys involving about six thousand persons.

The significance of these findings lies in the fact that in many northern middle-sized and small communities most majority-group adults have relatively little contact with minority-group members. Consequently, there is little opportunity for establishing communication and a felt relationship across racial lines. In one upstate New York community that we studied intensively, half of an adult cross-section of the majority-group population had no contact with any Negro, Jew, or Italian American at work, in the neighborhood, or in organizations. Another quarter had contact with only one of these groups in one of these situations.

There is a reason for this: In their daily activities, most people develop a sort of beaten path that they tread from home to work, then back home, then to lodge meeting, back home, on Sundays to church and back, and then perhaps a visit to close relatives or friends. Then the pattern is repeated. People stay on their beaten paths and only once in a while get off into the "forest," where all the rest of the hustle and bustle of urban life takes place. For most, the beaten path is a narrow walk of life that exposes them to just a few social environments and few contacts with people different in race, color, and creed.

Because of this narrow range, most persons lack real experience with members of minority groups. But lack of experience does not prevent them from forming misconceptions or impressions about these groups. If intergroup contacts occur and the minority persons do not fit these impressions, the participants are likely to experience discomfort and uneasiness. Minority-group members are uneasy where they are not sure they are accepted or wanted. Majority-group persons are uneasy when they are not sure (1) how they personally feel about interacting with minority persons in a particular situation; (2) how others present feel about interacting in the situation; (3) what behavior is expected in handling the situation; or (4) how the minority persons will react to this behavior. Such uneasiness is invariably communicated back and forth, even though surface talk and behavior appear quite normal and pleasant.

The uneasiness of mixed situations exerts a pressure on people to associate mostly with persons of their own group. People of the same background, locale, or origin generally mix together, anyway, and form common interests, like cultural traits, and mutual ties of acquaintance, friendship, and affection. These common bonds perpetuate "associational inbreeding" and cut down contacts with outgroups. In disadvantaged minorities, associational inbreeding is reinforced by the avoidance patterns that form after minority-group members have experienced rebuffs from the majority. They develop a sort of defensive insulation that protects them against further rebuff.

Where interaction does occur between minority and majority, the minority person tends, by a process of protective selection, to develop close contacts only among the more accepting majority members. Thus people who do associate together across group lines are, in the first place, usually more favorably disposed toward and more understanding of one another. This short-circuits somewhat the effectiveness of contacts in providing lines of communication for the inexperienced. Therefore, communities that, on the surface, seem to have "good situations" or "no racial problems" usually contain a mosaic of isolated subgroups, separated from one another by walls of misunderstanding, misconception, lack of contact, and lack of ability to communicate across group boundary lines on the rare occasions when contacts do occur.

PROPOSITION 2: *Persons inexperienced in intergroup relations frequently alienate minority persons with whom they wish to be friendly by inadvertently expressing themselves in the language of prejudice.*

A common cause of breakdown in communication across ethnic lines is what we have termed the "language of prejudice." Over the last decade or so it has become increasingly unfashionable to appear prejudiced, even in private conversation. Many inexperienced majority-group persons have become aware of some of the gross epithets that offend minority groups, such as "nigger," "kike," or "wop." "I don't like the Jews" has become "Some of my best friends are Jews." "I wouldn't want a Negro in my neighborhood" has become "Now, mind you, I'm not prejudiced, but you wouldn't want them on your doorstep, would you?" Or, "I don't mind, but my neighbors would object." Some southerners have altered the epithet "nigger" to "nigra." But many persons who may be aware of the gross errors in intergroup communication are often quite unaware of the hundred-and-one other mannerisms of speech and behavior that disturb communication between the groups.

It is, of course, no permanent solution to the problem of communication to try to avoid intergroup contact. A more realistic approach, in addition to increasing one's insight and sensitivity to minority problems or having frank interracial discussions on the subject, is to learn what phrases and words may be offensive to minority members. It is then possible to eliminate the words and phrases rather than avoid the contact so essential to intergroup understanding. Let us review some of these words and phrases, ranging from little-noticed, careless expressions to stinging epithets, that raise such formidable barriers to communication.

1. *Phrases that pertain to color.*—These usually equate whiteness with purity or desirability and blackness with evil and, therefore, by implication, are insulting to Negroes: "free, white, and twenty-one," "he treated me white," "things look pretty black," or the seemingly magnanimous: "Your face may be black, but your heart is as white as mine."

2. *Testimonials to the minority.*—Sometimes a white person who genuinely wants to be liked and accepted by Negroes tries to prove lack of prejudice by assuring a Negro that "you're as good as I am," "I like your people," or "I've loved the colored ever since I was rocked to sleep in the arms of my black mammy." Such testimonials are usually motivated by the white person's earnest, well-intentioned desire to separate himself from the prejudiced, discriminating segment of the white community, to indicate to the Negro that "I'm not like the rest." But, despite good intentions, testimonials are annoying to

many minority-group members. Frequently the coolness that the testimonial evokes comes as a surprise to the well-meaning person who delivers it, as in the following incident:

A group of individuals who were attending a joint conference were watching the 1952 Republican party convention on television. The animated conversation among them centered around the convention, which at the moment was polling votes for Eisenhower and Taft.

One of them, a white Protestant minister, decided to strike up a conversation with a Jewish delegate seated next to him. He cleared his throat rather audibly and said, "Say, wasn't that rabbi who addressed our institute yesterday a terrific speaker?" The Jewish delegate gave no response, except a vague, "Oh, yes." So the minister continued: "I do think rabbis are wonderful scholars. They are so much more dedicated, so much more eloquent in their faith, than many of us in the Protestant ministry." The Jewish delegate merely nodded politely at the minister and turned back to watch television. There the conversation ended.

What happened here? Since the conversation and attention of the group centered around the political convention, the minister's opening remark seemed extraneous and forced to the Jewish delegate and appeared to be directed to him primarily because he was Jewish, not because it was a conversational topic of established common interest. Furthermore, this statement and the one that followed appeared exaggerated and patronizing. The Jewish delegate knew from his own experience that not all Jewish rabbis were great scholars and equally that Protestant ministers could not be characterized by one or two glib phrases. He felt that the minister was much more aware of him as a Jew than as an individual. The minister, on the other hand, intended his remarks to convey his good will toward Jews. He was nonplused when the comments did not succeed either in opening the conversation or in calling forth a warm response from the Jewish delegate that would get their relationship off to a good start.

Exaggerated remarks often sound patronizing, and mature individuals resent them. If a majority-group person strikes up a conversation with a member of a minority group in terms of some common interest rather than something that calls attention to minority status, the response is usually better. After all, minority members, in addition to their interest and concern about intergroup relations, also share the same interests and concerns as other people in our society. Minority-group members, hearing an exaggerated testimonial to the virtues of their group, have difficulty realizing that the other person may be sincere in his protestations. Effective practitioners in intergroup relations try to find opportunities in the normal course of their relationships with such well-meaning persons to indicate that less race-oriented ways of showing friendship and respect are much more convincing to most minority-group members.

3. *Disparagement of other minorities.*—Sometimes a white person talking with Negroes feels free to disparage another minority, such as the Jews or Catholics, without realizing that his listeners may object. Minority persons increasingly believe that they are all in the same boat and that situations that are disadvantageous to one minority are bad for all. Actually, the scientific evidence we have shows that persons prejudiced against one group are likely to be prejudiced against other groups. Negroes often conclude that if a white Gentile has disparaged Jews to him, he will disparage Negroes to Jewish acquaintances.

4. *Caricatures of minority persons.*—From time to time, public programs of one kind or another exaggerate or burlesque supposed characteristics of a minority group. Most frequent are the blackface minstrel shows that exaggerate the lip and eye characteristics and speech mannerisms of the Negro and impute a degrading stupidity to him. Motion-picture, television, and radio types like Stepin Fetchit, Amos 'n' Andy, and Beulah spread these caricatures as though they applied to all Negroes. Similar caricatures of Jews, Italians, and other national and religious minorities appear from time to time. Not all members of the minority object to them, of course, but a

substantial number do, and if they hear a majority person praising or laughing about them, they may resent it.

Frequently these caricatures get embodied in comic strips or picture postcards that show Negroes as "handkerchief heads," "black mammies," and pickaninnies; Jews as sharp operators with derby hats and big noses; Italians as organ-grinders; and so on. Souvenir shops frequently sell trinkets or toys that show Negroes eating watermelon, shrieking at ghosts, or disappearing into alligators. In different forms, these caricatures may be brought unthinkingly into the home or office, for minority-group members to see and to interpret as evidence of prejudice or, at the least, insensitivity.

5. *Prejudgments and stereotypes.*—Stereotypes are a crystallization of the misconceptions and peculiar notions that grow up about a group of unfamiliar people. We hear people say that the Jews are "pushy" or that they are "sharp operators in their business dealings." Many people believe that most Negroes are "lazy and ignorant," "childlike," "happy-go-lucky," and well satisfied with "just the simple things of life—and a bottle of gin for Saturday night." Mexicans are thought by some to have "something in their nature" that causes them to commit crimes of violence. Orientals are said to be "sly and untrustworthy."

At one time, because of the humble origins of many minorities in this country, there were some folkways or group customs that gave rise to these oversimplified characterizations. Although certainly they cannot now be applied with accuracy to these groups, still many of them persist and are the currency in which misconceptions about minorities circulate today. For example:

A settlement director (white, in this instance) was asked to provide some entertainment at a social held at the Negro church. He decided to take along a number of children, both Negro and white, from his after-school program. Many of the children were quite talented dancers. In introducing the children to his Negro audience, the settlement director said in a very friendly manner, all smiles, and with the best intentions in the world of conveying his warm feeling about the Negro children, "I'm happy to present to this audience a group of children from our settlement program. Our colored children have music in their feet you know, and make wonderful dancers." Although this remark was greeted with a patter of audience applause, a number of people frowned, to the surprised dismay of the settlement director.

A stereotype remains a stereotype, even if it seems favorable to the minority it describes. The stereotypic thinker reveals to the minority person a lack of acquaintance with the minority group and an apparent unwillingness to meet and deal with each member of the minority as an individual. As one Negro said, "Why should they expect *me* to be able to dance? All Italians aren't Carusos!"

Stereotypic thinking that lumps the whole minority together is probably responsible for the practice some people have of referring to Negroes as "Sambo," "Rastus," or "George." Names originally attached to the most oppressed, impotent, and obsequious Negroes have been picked up and used as convenient labels for all Negroes, on the assumption that they all are—or should be—shuffling and hat-in-hand.

Sometimes even favorable stereotypes can have unfortunate personal repercussions, as in this instance:

A white Protestant high-school teacher was fond of saying: "I just *assume* that the Jewish students will make the honor roll and the dean's list. We never have more than four or five Jewish students in my class, and invariably they *do* get on the honor roll. Whenever I have a Jewish student who does only fair-to-middling work, I know that the student isn't working up to capacity. I always talk to those Jewish students for I know they can do better."

One Jewish boy, an average student, was pressed so hard by this teacher that he left school in his junior year to join the Navy and said that he felt he "had let down the Jewish people" as well as his teacher by not making the honor roll.

Historic circumstances, such as the talmudic tradition of scholarship and the denial to eastern European Jews of educational opportunities, have led many Jews to see education as the unfailing "open sesame" to prestige and worldly goods.

Jewish parents, more often than not, place high importance on their children's educational achievement. But this is not the same thing as saying that "all Jewish children are brilliant" and, by virtue of birth alone, are automatic candidates for scholastic honors.

6. *The ethnic joke.*—Our culture abounds with comic stories in dialect about Jews, Negroes, and various groups of foreign extraction. The minority person is not always the butt of the joke and frequently comes off in superior form. Many of the jokes are exceedingly funny. But because it is so difficult to tell who will resent them and under what circumstances, members of the majority often offend minorities even when they have only the best intentions. Frequently the characteristics of one or another of the characters in the story are stereotypic or disparaging. The minority person cannot be sure whether the storyteller accepts or rejects the stereotypes he laughs about.

Sometimes a majority-group person is misled by the fact that minorities tell such stories among themselves, occasionally in the presence of an outsider. But it is far different from poking fun at one's self or one's own people to hear an outsider of unknown sentiments disparage the group.

7. *"Slips."*—A "slip" is the accidental use of an expression such as "I worked like a nigger," "I jewed him down," "dago red" (referring to wine), "There's a nigger in the woodpile," or in the popular song: "In the evening by the moonlight, you can hear those darkies singing." Among the more offensive of these songs is "Polly-Wolly-Doodle":

> I come to the river and I couldn't get across;
> I jumped on a nigger and I thought he was a hoss. . . .

Unfortunately, the mosaic of our culture is inlaid with these little phrases and clichés that are insulting to minorities. Most people use them in total unawareness of their ethnic significance. Some persons unthinkingly use expressions like "That was a real Christian thing to do" or "That's darn white of you" without even realizing that they are often offensive to others.

A part of our common parlance, stereotypes can slip into a person's talk before the inner censor can get out his scissors. Then suddenly, the "slip" is out, and there is the Negro or Jew or foreign-born person looking on with astonishment, hurt, or resentment.

In our actions, too, we sometimes show insensitivity by sending Christmas cards to Jewish friends, arranging a Friday conference lunch or dinner with Catholics present where the main dish is meat, inviting Jews who "keep kosher" to partake of food in our nonkosher homes, and so on.

8. *Intentional use of racial epithets.*—We all have heard references to "kikes," "shines," "wops," "dagoes," "chinks," "Japs," "jigaboos," "coons," "smokes." Some Negroes can recall as many as twenty or thirty such phrases that they have come across in their experience. Whereas the "slip" is accidental, the epithet is intentional. It is designed to sting, to hurt, to infuriate. And it does. It may be hard to understand why these racial epithets arouse such fury and anguish, but such expressions usually come at the top of the minority person's list of "What Makes Me Mad." There seems to be no parallel phrase that would call forth a similar response in a majority-group person. Slandering his mother is close, but not close enough. Epithets can precipitate fights, cause lawsuits, or sever lifelong friendships. Their seriousness can hardly be exaggerated.

The epithet excepted, there are great variations in minority reactions to breaches of the "etiquette" of intergroup communication. Some minority members are highly sensitive to all such breaches; some would resent them in an outsider and ignore them in a friend; some employ them when talking to others of their own group; some, with a low level of minority identification, ignore them completely. But anyone who thinks these considerations are not important in intergroup relations communication need only glance at the figures in Table 2. In a northeastern middle-sized city, a cross-section of 150 adult Negro respondents was asked: "Which of these things make you angry, which just annoy you, and which don't bother you at all?" The responses are given in Table 2 in percentages.

In addition, 44 per cent of the Negroes reported that they felt uncomfortable when a white person told them, "You're as good as I am," whereas only 23 per cent reported a positive reaction. When asked about deterrents to greater contact with white people, two-thirds mentioned one or more barriers. Of these, 50 per cent agreed that they expected the white person

TABLE 2

	Makes Me Angry (Per Cent)	Annoys Me (Per Cent)	Doesn't Bother Me (Per Cent)
When a white person tells you how much he likes Negroes (testimonial).....................	9	32	59
When a white person tells you how much he dislikes some other minority like the Jews (faulty rapport device)...........................	26	36	38
When a white person forgets or "slips" and uses the word "darky" (the "slip")...............	57	26	17
When a white person uses the word "nigger" (the intentional epithet)........................	74	15	11

to "make a 'slip' and say something bad about Negroes." Even among Negro youth, 43 per cent agreed with the extreme statement, "When I am around whites, I am *always* expecting someone to make a 'slip' and say something bad about Negroes."

There are some important implications of this language of prejudice that need further exploration. It is widely believed that the person with wisdom and experience in intergroup relations makes no distinctions as to race or religion but, instead, views Negroes or Jews or Mexicans as "just like anyone else." But if a person is encouraged to be sensitive and thoughtful about barriers to intergroup communication, doesn't that mean he must *constantly* keep in mind the race or religion of the other person so that he won't make a "slip"?

Not exactly. Many of the words and phrases of the language

of prejudice can be weeded out of common usage by the same training and expression of disapproval as are used to eliminate blasphemy and cursing. People rapidly learn what is taboo and what is not, especially if they violate the taboos in groups that disapprove. Most people with any extended experience in intergroup interaction are aware of the language of prejudice. But this experience is absolutely essential if a person is to develop ease, naturalness, and spontaneity in communication with members of other groups. The newcomer to an interracial setting is bound to make occasional mistakes, but if the feeling tone is good, they can be picked up by others and corrected without doing permanent damage to the relationship.

If inexperienced persons are made aware of the language of prejudice, repeated errors can be prevented. The more the newcomer to an intergroup setting is encouraged to be responsive to cues that indicate he may have transgressed, the more rapidly he will learn what offends and what does not. Spontaneous and relaxed communication comes when a person has learned the language of prejudice and, over a period of time, has eliminated from his vocabulary phrases and expressions that might be offensive to minority-group members. When these expressions are no longer part of a person's spontaneous speech habits, he need no longer constantly keep in mind the other person's minority status in order to be able to talk without offending him.

PROPOSITION 3: *Intergroup understanding is impeded by ignoring individual and group differences and treating all persons as though they were alike.*

In connection with the language of prejudice, we have already qualified somewhat the widely held "treat-everybody-alike" principle for solving intergroup problems. Here are some further qualifications.

For one thing, the principle ignores real differences in customs and beliefs that have solid roots in the subculture of the minority. Jews certainly do have different religious observances and beliefs, and these frequently do lead to quite different eating practices and food habits and affect their social interaction with members of the out-group in certain situations. It would be highly unrealistic to ignore these differences. Just as schools make allowances for absences on Jewish holidays, so skilful practitioners in intergroup relations manage situations so that cultural differences of this sort are taken for granted and provided for. This will prevent them from becoming a source of embarrassment to either minority or majority.

Second, the treat-everybody-alike method ignores the fact that the minority person may bring to the interactive situation an emotional outlook conditioned by bitter and unpleasant experiences. The sting of repeated indignities sometimes produces a general bitterness that complicates the minority person's reaction to intergroup situations. The sympathetic understanding on which genuine communication depends is often delayed by overlooking the real facts of minority experience.

Finally, the treat-everybody-alike principle assumes that there are no cultural differences worth acknowledging and preserving in the life of the minority group. Intercultural programs often make much of the contributions of each of our different ethnic groups to our society. It is difficult to appraise how much these contributions are due to "differences" from one group to another. But certainly the preservation and encouragement of different art forms, religious observances, foods, or even speech patterns is no more incompatible with our way of life than the many differences we encourage in recreational and leisure-time pursuits. Only when these differences become the butt of invidious comparisons and scapegoating are they a source of friction.

The principle of equal treatment for all was originally intended to mean that everyone should receive equally fair and understanding treatment, regardless of race, creed, or national origin. To some practitioners *equal* treatment has come to

mean the *same* treatment. This interpretation tends to reinforce the feeling of many persons involved in intergroup relations work that special skills or training are unnecessary. "After
all, race relations are human relations and if we really understand human beings, we will know how to work with *all* hu-

TABLE 3

THE MORE EFFECTIVE AND TRAINED WORKER IS MORE LIKELY
TO HAVE REALISTIC ATTITUDES TOWARD MINORITY GROUPS

	Trained Worker on Staff and Judged More Effective (Per Cent)	Trained Worker on Staff and Judged Less Effective, or No Trained Worker on Staff and Judged Effective (Per Cent)	No Trained Worker on Staff and Judged Less Effective (Per Cent)
Total cases.................	30	85	126
Which . . . do you feel *predominates* in your attitudes during your day-to-day work on the job:			
"Negroes are just like other people; we should react to them just as to anyone else and *not* as Negroes"....................	53	65	68
"Because Negroes have had rebuffs and disadvantages as a minority, we should be aware of the difference being a Negro makes"....................	47	35	32
	100	100	100

man beings, regardless of race, creed, or color." This is an ap-
pealing and comforting thought. Of course, Negroes are human
beings, whites are human beings, and Negro-white relationships are human relationships. But genuinely equal treatment
comes from recognizing real ethnic-group differences, so that
each individual can be understood in the context of his own
ethnic traditions and experiences.

As shown in Table 3, better-trained and more effective practitioners[2] are more likely to be aware that equality of treatment does not necessitate treating everybody alike. Rather, they take into consideration the unique experiences of minority persons when relating to them.

2. See chap. 4, particularly nn. 1 and 2.

CHAPTER 3

Minority Participation in Policy
and Program[1]

PROPOSITION 4: *An effective intergroup relations program generally requires adequate minority representation among those who develop and guide the activities of the organization.*

Because of real differences in minority- and majority-group experience and the real barriers to communication that exist in most community settings, practitioners in intergroup relations must handle mixed situations with great sensitivity and understanding. This understanding involves alertness to both minority and majority perceptions of many situations and usually requires constant interpretation by persons much closer to minority experience than the average nonminority worker. This makes it essential to have participating in any program minority persons with keen understanding of minority experience.

It is essential also because it demonstrates that the agency "means business" in intergroup relations. If an organization does not actually involve minority members in its program, it is always open to the charge that it does not really mean what it says about integration. Therefore, the more overt specific instances of integration the community can "see" in the agency program, the better the agency indicates its sincerity.

In recent years, many intergroup agencies have passed through a series of stages in their opinions about minority participation, from (1) a belief that minorities should not be represented in policy-making discussions ("Naturally, we cannot discuss their problems while they are sitting there") to (2) a

1. This chapter was written in collaboration with Robert B. Johnson (see p. 7, n. 1).

belief that minority participation is acceptable *only* in order that a representative may be the spokesman for "his people" to (3) a belief that the minority representative is a responsible community member, able to make decisions affecting the total program of the agency. But even though the minority representative may justly prefer to be considered first as a community representative and only secondarily as a spokesman for a minority group, there are nevertheless several specific contributions he can make because of his minority-group membership. Let us consider briefly some of the important functions such persons can perform:

a) They can serve as a factual resource for providing information about minority life (e.g., a Jewish member might point out that the big program planned for next month falls on a Jewish holiday; a Negro member could report that several mothers of teen-age girls in the Negro community felt that there were no respectable places where their daughters could go dancing on dates). However, it is sometimes assumed by majority-group persons that, just because a person is a Negro, he will know every last detail about every Negro in a community numbering thousands of people. Such an assumption is, of course, unrealistic. And it is easy for majority-group persons to fall unwittingly into the habit of turning to these particular minority representatives as final authorities on matters of fact and opinion that are highly controversial.

b) They can help to interpret the diversity of minority life. Persons with little experience in intergroup situations are sometimes inclined to say, "I thought the Jews felt this way about Christmas pageants," or "Don't Negroes realize there's no malice in minstrel shows?" The minority persons can then explain (and may have to continue week after week to explain until the point "takes") that some Jews feel this way, some that way, some have still a third reaction.

c) They can also interpret "shortcomings" of the minority as judged by various majority members. Without understanding the roots of minority experience, the majority person who is trying to do something in intergroup relations may occasionally feel "They are so impractical," "Those leaders have a chip on their shoulders," "They don't show any ambition to better themselves," "They have such an apathetic devil-may-care attitude," "Why is it that they all live in such shabby homes, and yet they all drive Cadillacs and Buicks?" etc. There are reasons for minority reactions of various kinds, and minority persons who know this are often able to interpret them to majority-group persons so that insightful understanding replaces an initial superficial reaction.

d) They can also be an invaluable aid in interpreting minority sensitivity to incidents. Sometimes some minor rebuff, such as not including any Negro girls in a school or settlement play, will stir up a tempest that seems to the whites to be far out of proportion to the apparent importance of the incident. The minority person can perhaps show how the incident aroused and focused the anger that had accumulated from a long series of rebuffs that the minority group had absorbed.

Despite these cogent reasons for having minority participation, leaders with little experience in intergroup relations may show considerable timidity and reluctance to inaugurate minority participation at the top levels of policy and program. The most commonly stated objections to bringing minority persons into the staff or leadership of a social agency or community organization appear to be the following:

"We are not ready for it." "Readiness," however, does not develop automatically out of a vacuum. The members may need a series of frank discussions to explore their feelings and reactions to what initially may appear to them a radical suggestion. The important thing is for a board to avoid hiding for years behind the phrase "We are not ready," as a rationalization for lack of movement. The sensitive executive may need considerable insight into the thinking of his board members to determine what really motivates the "not ready" statement.

"We won't be able to talk freely." Some leaders in organizations that have intergroup programs tend to think of themselves as the "privileged" who are acting on behalf of the "underprivileged" people across the tracks. They sometimes have difficulty relating to minority persons on an equalitarian give-and-take basis. Many social service organizations and recreational centers began at a time when social service work was viewed as "charity" and was initiated and administered by ladies and gentlemen of leisure. This tradition persists in many places. It is easy to understand how a homogeneous board of the social elite would put a high value on personal compatibility and perhaps even feel that success in operation depends on the harmony that grows out of their being members of the same economic class or social circle or even of the same church or neighborhood. To introduce ethnic and class differences may even appear to them to be divisive and disruptive. They reason that it would be more difficult to be relaxed and spontaneous —and there would be more chance of hurting someone's feelings.

But differences can be creative as well as divisive. It is the function of the professional, faced with a homogeneous leadership situation, to make use of minority participation to bring about among the leaders a less patronizing and more genuine understanding of minority problems. Amiability merely for the sake of amiability does not guarantee movement; it may even inhibit progress. In the long run, professional intergroup relations programs benefit by exposing board members and other leaders to persons who are "different." It is precisely out of the experience of learning to discuss intergroup problems with an understanding of the feelings of minority people whose life-experience, values, and reactions differ that the majority-group person becomes sensitized to the dimensions of intergroup relations that affect the entire organization.

"Why should we pioneer?" This objection is sometimes expressed by leaders who are concerned about getting too far ahead of the rest of the community. They may be afraid they cannot interpret integration to friends or to colleagues who may look with disfavor on the initiation of minority participation. But evidence is accumulating that an agency often can move quite forthrightly toward an integration objective if it believes in it, without having to be oversensitive to what other agencies practice (see chap. 5).

Groups differ in their readiness to move forward and pioneer. The chief danger, however, is that the agency program may become completely dormant, with no effort made to involve different kinds of people in the membership, staff, or board. In such circumstances, the desire not to "pioneer" becomes an ostrich-like head-in-the-sand policy.

One group-work agency in a fair-sized northeastern community called together other lay and professional leaders to discuss its own desire to advance intergroup relations and to find out whether there were others wanting to do the same. Other agencies that had been hesitant in this regard were encouraged by the action of the first agency. They, too, had thought they were "pioneers" in even thinking about the problem. With this bit of initiative and some subsequent discussions, agencies that had thought they were "pioneering," alone in their efforts, found support from other groups that had been blocked by the same kind of isolated "lone-wolf" thinking.

"They don't have qualified leaders." When a minority community is small, it is sometimes genuinely difficult to find the minority leaders one would like. Acutely conscious of the generally lower educational level of some minorities, some leaders reject minority participation by taking refuge in the seeming difficulty of finding college graduates, people of middle-class background, or people who have demonstrated community leadership and responsibility.

Since there are many different types of leaders in different ethnic groups, the majority-group person is seriously handicapped in recognizing or even being aware of the existence of "leaders" within specific nationality and racial groups. A certain settlement-house board in a small midwestern community was lamenting the lack of "qualified" personnel among the Spanish-American and Puerto Rican people in the local community. When the name of Mr. X., a bartender in the Puerto Rican community, was mentioned, there were raised eyebrows on the board, and one disconcerted member asked, "Who ever heard of a bartender serving on a board committee?"

Another board member, a member of the Woman's Christian Temperance Union, was particularly distressed that a bartender was even being considered for membership on a board committee. Yet this particular bartender was a natural leader in the minority community. Youngsters went to see him for help in finding jobs. He loaned money to teen-agers attending trade school and was a trusted counselor to many families. This person enjoyed high respect in his own community and was noted for his honesty and integrity. He could have been an invaluable aid to the settlement. He could give a feeling of trust and confidence in the settlement to many people because of the trust and confidence placed in him. Yet, because the board of this settlement looked upon bartending as an unacceptable occupation, a natural community leader was lost to the program.

Many minority communities have not yet developed a substantial group of middle-class leaders, such as businessmen able to take time off from their businesses or housewives with ample leisure time. Majority-group leaders who have all their lives dealt only with middle-class, professional, or white-collar people need help in learning to recognize natural leadership, whether it is garbed in overalls, a business suit, or a bartender's apron.

If the "natural" leaders are not the conventional leading citizens (who may be "prominent" but may exercise no real functional leadership), then how does one locate this new type of leader? One way we have found helpful is to ask various knowledgeable people in the minority community—such as ministers, officers of parent-teacher associations and women's clubs, or schoolteachers—to identify the "natural" leaders. They will know whose opinions are sought out on important issues within the minority community, who helps people with personal problems, such as finding a job, borrowing money, or getting a son into college. In a minority community of several thousand, a few persons' names will be mentioned over and over again; they will probably be the "natural" leaders. The point here is that finding them requires some systematic investigation.

"Mr. So-and-So will resign from the board or refuse to contribute financially if we try to push this thing too fast." Sometimes this is a realistic price that has to be paid for intergroup relations progress. But experience shows that threats of this sort are rarely carried out if adequate interpretation is given, perhaps with demonstration of the workability of integration in other agencies. More often than not, such objections reflect primarily the uncertainty, fear, and anxiety attendant on a new situation where experience is lacking. The professional's job is to work with that anxiety as a leverage point for bringing the majority person to a new level of intergroup understanding.

One able executive, faced with a board member who seriously threatened the progress of the agency's intergroup relations program, invited him to visit a board meeting of another local agency that had an integrated board. Over a period of years this agency had worked with several minority leaders who were articulate, able, and devoted to agency principles. The visiting board member was surprised to see Negro and white women freely and equally discussing the business and program of their agency. It was a new experience for him to witness a free give-and-take and to see mutual respect among people who differed in race and national origin.

This one visit did not convert the doubting board member. It did give him food for thought. It indicated to him that a board and an agency program could be integrated without sacrificing mutual respect and good feelings. These modest learning experiences are important for many community leaders whose daily routines insulate them from contact with large numbers of persons of different social and religious backgrounds.

Some executives are inclined to feel that, once a minority person has been taken in on the policy or leadership level, "integration" or "representativeness" has somehow miraculously been achieved. Note the remark of one social agency president: "Mrs. X. has been a perfectly lovely Negro woman on our board. She agrees with everything that is done, co-operates beautifully, and never causes any difficulty. We really have a representative and integrated board." This particular agency had made modest headway in developing its intergroup relations program. A Negro woman had finally been placed on the board as a representative of the minority community. But she had few leadership abilities and was so flattered at being asked on the board that she spent most of her time being friendly, polite, and courteous. The board members liked this behavior; it flattered their egos, sustained their feelings of superiority, and tacitly acknowledged the real social distance that separated them from the Negro board member. It also satisfied them that they were really democratic and were really "doing something" about the race problem.

Actually, token representation of this sort may do more harm than good. The Negro community may have the impression that the point of view of the minority is getting a hearing and that important information about its conditions of life and its reactions is being brought to the attention of the agency. But if a representative does not have keen understanding of minority problems and their relationship to the majority, little interpretation to the majority can take place. And if the minority representative is timid or awed by the economic status or social standing of the elite, he may have great difficulty in trying to communicate the insights he does have. Meanwhile, the majority leaders comfort themselves with the illusion of being democratically in touch with the minority community. The principle here is:

PROPOSITION 5: *Fullest minority participation in planning policy and program involves the participation of minority persons with insight into minority problems, skills in social relationships with persons of different social and ethnic status, articulateness in discussing minority majority relations, and the emotional poise to handle touchy subjects and situations without becoming bitter or hostile.*

This seems like a big order, since it requires mature and friendly persons who have a feeling of ease in confronting the majority group with delicate matters and a feeling of comfort in having psychologically worked through their own minority-group feelings. Although, at first, minority representatives like this may be put in the position of dealing almost exclusively with minority interpretation, soon, if they have real leadership ability, they will take their place in the program, work for the purposes of the organization as a whole, and make their contribution accordingly. Minority participation is full-fledged only when the minority person participates fully in discussion and decision-making, has confidence and ease in his status in the group, and feels his opinions and point of view are respected in matters other than minority-majority relations alone.

Because of the danger of "token representation," effective minority participation is rarely achieved with fewer than two minority persons. The presence of two persons can give extra protection against inadequate minority representation in these ways:

a) A minority member will less easily retire into silence, deference to status, or polite acquiescence if he must maintain his role as a champion of minority rights in the eyes of a fellow minority member.

b) The minority members can reinforce each other in interpreting positions they take.

c) Differences of opinion among minority members give meaning to the variations within the minority group and make it more likely that a position will be accepted on its merits rather than because "our representative from the Negro community says so."

Because of the seriousness of the problem of token representation and the wide variations in point of view and maturity among minority leaders, great care should be given to the selection of minority representatives in the light of their roles and status in the minority community.

In the typology that follows, an attempt is made to analyze different types of minority leadership. Any typology that applies to people is misleading because it oversimplifies and almost caricatures in bold terms characteristics that, when found in real life, are complex and intermingled with many other personality variables. It is especially dangerous to use typologies of this sort as labels to apply to real people, since the label may easily blind one to other characteristics that do not fit the "type." Besides, persons change and show personal growth and react differently in new situations. Minority representatives especially are subject to change under pressure from the minority community or under the weight of new responsibilities of leadership. However, with these cautions in mind, let us scan quite briefly some of the different "types" of leaders that are found in Negro communities across the country. (Although these types were derived primarily from the study of Negro communities, parallel types are certainly present in many other minorities.)

1. *The "Uncle Toms."*—One of the most derogatory expressions used among Negroes to characterize servile, obsequious, and ingratiating behavior among other Negroes is the phrase "Uncle Tom." Sometimes such a person is called "a white man's Negro," because he is thought to be more interested in carrying

out the interests and desires of the majority group than in expressing the needs and aspirations of his own people. The "Uncle Tom" is usually overly polite, constantly smiling, and fearful of alienating what he perceives as the omnipotent majority group. These attitudes are probably a cultural carry-over from the days of slavery, when ingratiation was often the slave's only safe method of improving his lot. But today respect for "Uncle Tom" and his supposed "influence" with the majority group is fast disappearing as minority groups increase their economic independence, social status, and self-respect. Among representatives of the race the occasional "Uncle Tom" is the person most likely to give the minority only token participation, and even this may be misleading because he is often so thoroughly repudiated by the minority community. And because the "Uncle Tom" is most likely to be known to white leaders unfamiliar with the Negro community, he is most likely to be chosen in those situations where the need for more representative leadership is most important.

2. *The "militant hostile" (or "hostile aggressive") leader.*—Most minority communities contain a few leaders whose bitterness and anguish over their own past minority experience or that of others causes them to seem chronically hostile and aggressive toward any member of the majority group. They remember vividly all the injustices and hurts suffered by their people and are determined that the majority group shall be continually reminded of them. Though their strong and unwavering militancy is often a significant and valuable impetus to the minority community, their aggressiveness and sensitivity may sometimes lessen their personal effectiveness in influencing policy and program and in interpreting minority problems. Their behavior may often seem immoderate and unreasonable to the majority-group member, who prefers a more polite type of minority representative. They sometimes become constructive and useful participants only after they have "tested" the

majority members and become assured of their sincerity and good faith.

3. *The "interracial duty delegate."*—In many Negro communities we find an overworked interracial representative who dutifully undertakes to be present when a "Negro" is wanted. Frequently, he will be the only brown face, and he is likely to be viewed by the majority group (and to perceive himself) as spokesman for the whole minority. Because he is ever present and ever willing to serve, majority-group members are understandably tempted to rely on him as the major spokesman for the Negro community and not explore further to insure broader representation, though he may actually represent only one segment of it.

4. *The "shy mouse."*—An occasional inarticulate and reticent minority member finds himself, perhaps unwillingly, in the role of minority representative. Coming perhaps from a modest working-class background and suffering the handicaps of an incomplete education, he is likely to be overawed by the social standing and articulateness of other participants. As minority representative, he is seriously hampered in expressing his point of view and that of other minority persons and in winning support for his position.

5. *The "whitewardly mobile status striver."*—Occasionally a Negro who is ambitious socially and economically will come to value association with white persons of high status because of the prestige it involves in his own eyes and often in the eyes of some of his own group. Memberships on committees and boards are feathers in his cap; they are things to be cultivated and maintained. Such a person will be inclined to work hard at being pleasant and acceptable, but to shy away from situations that might threaten his standing in the majority group. Consequently, it becomes difficult for him to confront the majority with situations that might call forth antagonism or hostility. In addition, he may be mobile away from the minority

community and thus not be an adequate representative for it. For example:

> In one women's organization, the board had started the policy that all members of the agency, regardless of race, color, or creed, should use its swimming pool. The staff member in charge of the swimming pool implemented this policy decision in a peculiar way. She merely scheduled different swimming periods for different nationality and racial groups and thus created a segregated condition. She justified this condition as "realistic" and at least obedient to the strict letter of the law of the board's policy decision. Of course, it was a violation of the spirit of the board's policy, which was simultaneous use of the pool by different groups. One of the minority-group girls complained about this situation to the minority-group board member, asking her to bring it to the attention of the board for remedial action. The board member found it most difficult to do so for fear of alienating or embarrassing her fellow board members. Above all else, she prized their friendship on the board.

In such instances, stress on amiability, friendliness, and currying majority-group favor causes the whitewardly mobile person to lose sight of larger intergroup objectives in favor of personal conditions.

6. *The "friendly-but-firm" workers for equality.*—We use this term to describe minority representatives who are militant but reasonable, whose militancy is adjusted to the present situation rather than to more tense and undemocratic past situations. They feel keenly the necessity of participating and contributing as community members as well as minority-group members; they also feel keenly their responsibility to interpret the life-history and sentiments of other members of the minority community. They believe that only joint participation in social action, by both minority and majority groups, will guarantee progress toward intergroup objectives. They strive to implement a realistic intergroup program with a constancy that sometimes creates discomfort among others in the organization. But the "friendly militant" is a constructive co-worker precisely because he characteristically interprets conflicts over policy and practice as what they are and not, like the "militant hostile" leader, as a rejection of himself or his ethnic status.

The "friendly-but-firm" worker normally makes the best minority representative, because he can be militant and positive without permanently alienating or rejecting the persons who oppose him. Out of the conflict situation in which he participates grow relationships with majority-group persons that form the basis for effective joint action in the future.

Majority-group leaders sensitized to problems of communication across racial lines realize that only by understanding the life-history of the minority person and his range of psychological reactions to minority status, can they develop effective working relationships. They are aware that what may occasionally seem to be unreasonable minority-group hostility has roots in a lifetime of unequal treatment. They have learned to feel with the minority-group member what it is to be rejected, to be thought different and inferior, to be called names that are insulting, to be looked on as a second-class citizen and a second-class person. They see personal reactions of minority-group persons in part as differential reactions to minority status. Only as majority and minority leaders work intimately and conscientiously in an atmosphere of mutual respect and acceptance will they develop the friendly, firm, comfortable, self-respecting point of view that is needed to implement an effective intergroup relations program.

CHAPTER 4

A Staff Trained in Intergroup
Relations

It is probably clear from the preceding discussion that to
have successful intergroup relations involves much more than
just wanting to be friendly and democratic. All the good will
a person can muster will not in itself eliminate the language of
prejudice or provide insight into different types of minority
leaders. Yet many executives with intergroup relations programs have staff members who have never been trained in
these and many other intergroup relations matters. Since they
—more often than the executive himself—are on the "firing line"
in direct contact with members of both majority and minority
groups, volunteer workers, and members of the wider community, much of the success of an intergroup relations program
depends on the operating attitudes, knowledge, and skills of
the staff.

Staff members with little training or experience in this field
are quite likely to have a good deal of anxiety about their
adequacy in intergroup situations. They usually sense that all
is not right in their relationships, even though the overt clues
are few. The inexperienced white staff member may find himself struggling painfully with questions like the following:

Do the Negro children—and their parents—really trust me, or
do they think I'm just a "do-gooder" and not really sincere?

That was the first time I ever swam with a Negro and showered
with one. I wonder if he noticed that I felt uncomfortable.

I wonder if I'll ever get to the point where I won't think "Isn't
that just like a Negro!" whenever they do something that seems
typical.

I wonder whether they really like me. Sometimes I even wonder whether I really like *them.*

Thank heaven we haven't had any serious incidents for a while! But how long can we continue to hold our breaths in fear of incidents?

The inexperienced Negro worker will have much the same kind of anxiety, asking himself, perhaps:

How can I get across to those white staff members how patronizing they sound when they talk to Negro parents?

I wonder if the Negro people think I'm selling out because I go along with the director in so many things.

I sometimes get the feeling that all this intergroup relations stuff is just eyewash. They just want to talk big about it, make a few gestures, like hiring a Negro, then quit.

I wonder if the white staff members *really* like me. Sometimes they seem just a little *too* polite.

I sometimes get awfully discouraged. What's the use of it all? The white man is not going to change.

In both instances, white and Negro, the reactions are normal and understandable concomitants of situations wherein some barriers to communication still prevail and the differential reactions of the other group are not fully understood.

How can we break down existing barriers to communication within the staff and develop the understanding that the effective practitioner in intergroup relations requires? At times this must seem like an almost insurmountable task to executives who must, for financial and other reasons, use inexperienced staff workers fresh from academic halls. In instances like these, there is one big feature in the executive's favor: many new workers in intergroup relations come to the situation feeling that so long as they have friendly reactions to persons of all races and creeds, they have satisfied the main requirement for work in intergroup relations. Although we know that good will of this sort is not enough for effective work, it certainly is a foundation on which to build. The sheer eagerness of many young workers in intergroup relations to put the American Creed into practice gives the supervisor leverage with which to work.

Characteristics of Effective Staff Members

At this point it may be worth while to begin to specify what we might consider to be the characteristics of the effective intergroup relations practitioner. As an aid in doing this, let us look first at some of the responses of the executives of about four hundred recreational centers and settlement houses throughout the country. To get a comparison of the attitudes, programs, and thinking of the "superior" group-work programs with those of the "average" or perhaps "inferior" programs, the recreational centers were classified in two ways: (a) they were grouped into those that had one or more trained workers on the staff (e.g., with social work degrees)[1] and those that had none; and (b) they were classified by the staff of their national affiliates into those that were "most effective," "average," and "least effective," in their intergroup relations programs.[2] This gives six groups (see Table 4). Note that more of the centers with trained workers on the staff were judged "most effective."

1. The word "trained" as used in this study refers to "social work" training. The authors feel that social work education has developed a unique combination of theoretical training and supervised field work that provides a basic foundation for practice in the area of human relations. This is not meant to deny, of course, the value of training in related disciplines, such as recreation, nursery education, psychology, and education, which also provide educational and professional preparation for practice.

2. This classification process was as follows: The national staffs of two prominent social group-work agencies were given the names of all their professional workers listed individually on cards. There was no background data on the cards, except the name of the person and his agency. The card contained no data on education, training, or length of experience. The quality of performance of these workers was known to the national staffs through a variety of sources: field reports by the agency's regional director, personal visits by the national staff to the particular agency, and reports at national and regional conferences. The national staffs were asked to rate each worker according to his effectiveness in achieving the agency's intergroup relations goals. The ratings represented the combined opinion of the total national staff.

Then, for purposes of further comparison, we made three groupings:

a) Those with a trained worker *and* judged "most effective"
b) Those with *either* a trained worker *or* judged "most effective" *but not both*
c) Those with no trained workers on the staff and judged "average" or "least effective"

Some significant comparisons of the attitudes, perceptions, and program efforts of the directors of these three groups of centers are reported in Table 5; the central conclusions are summarized in boldface type within the table.

TABLE 4

Judged by Staff of National Affiliate as:	Trained Worker on Staff (Per Cent)	No Trained Worker on Staff (Per Cent)
"Most effective"	50	29
"Average"	29	32
"Least effective"	21	39
	100 (140 cases)	100 (216 cases)

TABLE 5

Item	Trained Worker on Staff and Judged More Effective	Trained Worker on Staff and Judged Less Effective, or No Trained Worker on Staff and Judged Effective	No Trained Worker on Staff and Judged Less Effective

Executives of agencies that have one or more social work trained workers on their staffs and are rated as more effective are more likely to have realistic responses to questions on attitudes toward minority groups

Per cent agreeing with the following statements:			
"Negroes are really a wonderful people—happy, generous, and eager to please"	24	48	64

TABLE 5—*Continued*

Item	Trained Worker on Staff and Judged More Effective	Trained Worker on Staff and Judged Less Effective, or No Trained Worker on Staff and Judged Effective	No Trained Worker on Staff and Judged Less Effective
"I genuinely feel that I am free of prejudice against Negroes".	67	79	78
"There are some Negroes that I just don't like".............	77	67	56
"Differences among groups, such as language differences, food preferences, or cleanliness habits, are matters which we should just accept or ignore because trying to interpret these things just calls attention to differences we are trying to minimize".....................	14	29	31
Total no. of cases................	30–63	78–113	112–38

Executives of agencies that have one or more social work trained workers on their staffs and are rated as more effective are less likely to project blame onto the minority group

Per cent agreeing with the following statements:			
"Sometimes I feel it's the Negroes' fault for not making more effort to co-operate with those of us who are trying to get a better deal for them"...	25	32	41
"We can't expect many Negroes to give mature leadership in the fight against discrimination, because they are much too self-involved to be objective about it"..............	3	24	32
Total no. of cases................	65–31	116–84	127–117
Per cent viewing "ineffective minority leadership in the community" as "very serious" or "fairly serious" in hampering good intergroup relations in their agency...............	63	69	72
Total no. of cases................	67	114	137

TABLE 5—*Continued*

Item	Trained Worker on Staff and Judged More Effective	Trained Worker on Staff and Judged Less Effective, or No Trained Worker on Staff and Judged Effective	No Trained Worker on Staff and Judged Less Effective

Executives of agencies that have one or more social work trained workers on their staffs and are judged effective differ from executives of other agencies in their perception of obstacles to good intergroup relations

Per cent viewing the following obstacles as "very serious" or "fairly serious" in hampering good intergroup relations in their agency:			
"Resistance or timidity by your board of directors"	21	37	36
"Unreasonable majority-group resentment against minority participation in program"	38	40	24
"The likelihood of opposition from the community in general"	47	49	35
Total no. of cases	58–68	111–15	135–37

Executives of agencies that have one or more social work trained workers on their staffs and are rated more effective are more likely to have done things that indicate an effort to integrate

Per cent saying they (or their staffs) have done the following things "frequently" or "a few times" during the past year:			
"Broken up a spontaneous all-white or all-Negro group in order to mix them"	39	23	15
"Met with a co-ordinating group representing clubs or activity groups to discuss intergroup relations in your agency"	70	71	59
"Set an example by having a mixed white and Negro group of friends meet socially in your house"	74	67	38
"Worked with a Negro youth to help him feel comfortable in a new situation with white members"	79	77	66
"Deliberately risked loss of some participation in order to promote better integration of Negroes in your agency program"	81	80	63
Total no. of cases	31–33	80–85	103–18

TABLE 5—*Continued*

Item	Trained Worker on Staff and Judged More Effective	Trained Worker on Staff and Judged Less Effective, or No Trained Worker on Staff and Judged Effective	No Trained Worker on Staff and Judged Less Effective

Executives of agencies that have one or more social work trained workers on their staffs and are judged effective differ from executives of other agencies in their opinions of which action efforts are effective

Per cent agreeing with following statements:			
"Pageants or festivals that dramatize the different cultural heritages of our children form a most effective way of achieving mutual understanding among children who differ in race, color, and creed"......	57	75	76
"We can't really accomplish much in the way of integrated activities until we find a way of reaching the parents—that's where the basic trouble is"...	45	50	56
Total no. of cases.................	65 67	115–110	138–124

Executives of agencies that have one or more social work trained workers on their staffs and are judged effective are more likely than executives in other agencies to report tension in their agency and to use tension incidents toward better relations

Per cent reporting one or more tension incidents in their agency during the last year or so..................	72	61	42
Total no. of cases.................	70	132	154
Per cent answering "frequently" or "a few times" to the following:			
"Deliberately made use of interracial incidents to broaden understanding across race lines".	61	61	51
Total no. of cases.................	33	84	97

On the basis of these and other findings, we have put together a profile of the effective professionals in intergroup relations as against what we might call the naïve, ineffective worker. This is not meant to set up a sharp line dividing intergroup relations practitioners into two identifiable groups. Most workers in the field undoubtedly have elements of both; but it may be helpful to set forth in bold outline some of the characteristics that are especially noticeable at either end of an imaginary continuum running from the ineffective worker of good will alone to the effective professional with training and experience in intergroup relations.[3] A rough comparison of the attitudes, knowledge, and skills of the effective professional with those of the less effective worker reveals the major differences shown below.

EFFECTIVE PROFESSIONAL	LESS EFFECTIVE PROFESSIONAL
Attitudes	
a) He is committed to a belief in the workability of integration and consciously devotes his efforts to achieving it	a) He is inclined to be passive and vague about objectives in intergroup relations, opportunistic in moving forward to goals, and willing to believe intergroup relations will improve of their own accord merely if he favors the American Creed
b) He accepts the limitations of the situation and people he must work with; he has a long-range view that is not easily discouraged	b) He tends to internalize or take personally the apathy, disinterest, and resistance he finds; he is inclined to be moralistic about "the minority not appreciating what we do for it"; he is patronizing and often critical of what he sees as their "personal limitations"

3. We do not mean to neglect those professional workers who, despite their lack of formal social work training, seem to have learned from their experiences alone and have become quite effective, able practitioners. These "naturals," however, as in most other professions, are in the mi-

EFFECTIVE PROFESSIONAL   LESS EFFECTIVE PROFESSIONAL
Attitudes (continued)

c) He is *person-centered* in his judgments of movement; he cares most what happens to individuals as a result of their intergroup experiences

c) He is *program-centered* in his judgment; he values the number of participants and the size of the program above the growth of individuals

d) He is aware of how his own background and experience have molded his own intergroup perceptions; he has insight into his own feelings and is aware of the ways his own prejudices are called forth; he does not deceive himself by thinking he is completely unprejudiced

d) He is inclined to think he is completely unprejudiced; he is not aware of the prejudices he has not worked through or how they color his reactions to intergroup situations

e) He is able to identify with and understand the reactions of the individual participants in his program regardless of their race and regardless of their prejudices; he appreciates the felt discomforts and prejudices of minority toward majority and majority toward minority

e) He is inclined to be sentimental in his reactions to the minority and critical or moralistic about both majority and minority prejudices; he thinks in terms of exaggerated, favorable stereotypes; he finds it difficult to individualize his personal relationships with different members of groups other than his own

Knowledge

a) He understands the nature of superficial prejudice, personality-rooted prejudice, and the mechanisms of scapegoating and exemption

a) He tends to confuse prejudice and personality characteristics and does not understand the relationships between them

b) He is aware of the wide diversity of minority experiences and knows what this means in terms of defensive

b) He does not appreciate the diversity and intensity of minority experience and is unaware of how many of the

nority. The great bulk of practitioners, the authors have found, benefit from social work training, especially from supervised field-work experience.

reactions, feelings of discomfort and morbidity, and differential reactions of minority persons to their status

"shortcomings" or "limitations" he perceives in minority persons are related to those experiences; he is inclined either to lump all minority persons together or to try to overlook the minority experience by viewing its members as "just like anyone else"

c) He understands the importance of friendly interaction and friendship formation across ethnic lines in reducing prejudice, and he works to increase interaction

c) He tends to assume the inevitability of acculturation and assimilation by the gradual wearing-away of prejudice through education and public enlightenment

d) He has sophisticated knowledge of the processes of social change in intergroup relations, such as how legal sanctions, authority, and social pressure can be used to achieve integration

d) He thinks of change in intergroup relations in terms of crude rules of thumb that hamper him in moving ahead; e.g., "We can't move any faster than the community," or "We won't make any real headway until we reach the parents"

e) He has knowledge about community and extra-community resources that can help him in his intergroup relations work

e) He tends to be insulated or isolated and to feel that his intergroup problems are unique

Skills

a) He can put a person at ease regardless of his group by relating to each person as an individual, but with sensitivity to that person's special minority or majority experiences; he is at ease himself in interactive situations

a) By making "slips," or using testimonials or stereotypes, he is likely to blunder in interactive situations and reveal his inexperience and lack of understanding of the problems of communication across ethnic lines; he is surprised and indignant when the reaction is negative to his utilization of testimonials as a friendship device

EFFECTIVE PROFESSIONAL	LESS EFFECTIVE PROFESSIONAL

Skills (continued)

b) He can interpret minority and majority experiences so that they increase the understanding of participants in interactive situations

b) He bypasses interpretation in favor of exhortation to ignore differences and "be one happy family"; he talks in generalities about "unity," "togetherness," "loving our fellow-man"

c) He can handle tension incidents so as to (1) give participants increased insight into themselves and other groups and (2) strengthen the climate of opinion for integration

c) He tends to perceive "incidents" as bad and to shy away from anything controversial that might lead to friction; he is confused and embarrassed by incidents and tends to play them down and avoid handling them

The Process of Maturation

The profile as described above expresses in summary form some of the things executives aim at when they try to pull together in their organizations a staff that can work effectively with majority and minority participants in their programs, with lay people on their boards, committees, and volunteer staffs, and with other community leaders. Much of the remainder of this book will discuss *how* this can be done. But, first, it might enhance our understanding of the process of maturation in intergroup relations to read the words of one young and rather inexperienced group worker about some of her own growing pains. Trained and experienced workers who have been in intergroup relations work for years sometimes forget to mention, or pass rather quickly over, the painful, seemingly endless, period of embarrassments, discomforts, soul-searchings, disappointments, anxieties, and thoughtful reflections that they went through as they matured in experience and understanding. This document, written by a young worker after attending her agency's training school, is a reminder of those experiences:

One can sit through all the lectures ever given on theoretical race relations and listen carefully to what is said. Outwardly you change because you realize before too long that it's the intelligent thing to do. You find yourself wanting to cry out, "No, that isn't true," when someone makes reference to a negative group stereotype, but you still catch yourself thinking, "Isn't that just like a ——!" when a person of a particular group does something that is generally considered characteristic of that group.

This is where I was after having spent four years in college learning the facts about group relations. I knew facts but couldn't apply them. For the most part the only Negroes I knew were those who fitted easily into the common stereotype. I was the "authority," the educated one, and to save myself I couldn't help feeling smug and superior.

At the training school I attended they helped me crystallize the idea that each man is valuable in and of himself—of the intrinsic worth of all men in the eyes of God. This was done in many ways—through discussion on personal security (assuming that you can't accept someone unlike yourself until you respect and are at peace with yourself). They taught us definite skills in leadership, discussion leading, sports, games and the like, all of which would be a help working directly with people. Many of the things we did so frequently that they soon became automatic. I think a definite effort was made at this so that they would come naturally when we were thrown into a group and could then give our whole mind to the individuals in the group rather than worrying about just what should be done next in terms of activity.

Through movies, panel discussion, and bull sessions we soon learned how it felt to be a Negro in this country, what it was like to come out of a meeting in New Orleans where Negroes and whites had been meeting together and then not be able to go home together because they couldn't sit together on the bus. It was definitely an emotional approach to the problem, but then, isn't the prejudice we feel in part an emotional response? We were able to see our directors, Negro and white women, working together in harmony, not always in complete agreement but disagreeing on an *equal level*. The staff was interracial. In our discussion groups, in our work groups, in our living arrangements, no differentiation was made because of race.

I had never eaten previously at a table with a Negro—I had never gone swimming with a Negro. I had never talked to a Negro girl about dating and marriage. Before long I realized that in hundreds of little ways we felt the same whether our skin was dark or light. For the first time in my life I was talking to and working with Negro women who had as good and in many cases a better educational background than I. I had to *admit* to myself that they knew what they were talking about—that as a beginner there was much I could learn from them, and I had to accept them on my own level. In spite of this I'm afraid that it was only rarely that I could listen to them and erase completely from my mind the preface "Negro." It still somewhat colored my evaluation of their conversation. Sometimes, even at the professional level, there was tension and resentment. However, we were all still learning. Sometimes I think we really learned precisely because we were free enough to express our hostility and anger. Without the facts that I had heard again and again, I don't believe I could have accepted the situation. Prejudice begins so early, it continues all during the period when we're not particularly critical or discriminating about what we hear or learn. It becomes a habit without our knowing it, so that, by the time any antiprejudice information is given us, our minds, which have become perhaps a little more critical, are somewhat inclined to think "If it's not true, how did it start in the first place?"

As I consider it now, it seems to me that the following should be one of the guideposts for group workers in the interracial field. We should never forget the struggle we have had within ourselves to reach a point where we accept a man as an individual rather than because of the fact that his skin is the same color as ours.

The people we are dealing with haven't for the most part had the benefit of our training. The road to acceptance is a long one and a hard one; it involves personal security and in many cases debunking a lifetime of wrong information and wrong attitudes.

Contact on a meaningful personal level seems to me many times more important than team play or sports. I played basketball in high school with and against Negro girls, but don't believe it changed my opinion of their race one iota.

Frankly, I am still uncomfortable about physical contact—I have to think deliberately about it in order to be casual or make it seem that way. Working with kids as I do, this is a definite drawback— when we play games in clubs it's important that I show no feelings about whether my partner for a particular event is black or white or pink or gray. They're kids who are there to have a good time and are people above all else. I am discovering that where I am accepted by a group of Negro girls, where I'm told their confidences and ideas freely, where I feel part of the group rather than a leader outside, I can step beyond many of my doubts and fears.

From this document and others like it, we can begin to discern delicate stages in the development of intergroup understanding and effectiveness. These might tentatively be described as follows:

1. *The negative phase.*—Persons in the negative phase characteristically have little or no contact with minorities, but they have picked up some of the negative stereotypes about them and are inclined to express negative attitudes about associating with them. Their general prejudice level reflects the cultural milieu in which they are currently participating, with a strong carry-over from earlier social environments.

2. *The "awakening" phase.*—Persons in the middle phases usually have contact with minorities and a generally favorable reaction to these contacts. But such reactions are likely to be characterized by one or more symptoms revealing that the person has not yet reached intergroup maturity. A common occurrence in this intermediate phase is the *exemption mechanism.* When a person's prejudice is relatively superficial and he is friendly and sociable with most of his associates, an appropriate and acceptable contact with a friendly minority-group member will generally call forth friendly reactions to the minority person. The majority person brings into the interaction the appropriate social patterns he has learned for interacting with others of his own group. These patterns, in turn, are the cues for further friendly interaction. In this way friendship formation may proceed quite naturally within the limits of that situation, seemingly at variance with an individual's expressed prejudices. The individual handles this inconsistency via the *exemption mechanism,* that is, he exempts this minority member from the general prejudice he holds, on the ground, say, that this particular Jew (or Negro) is superior to and different from most Jews (or Negroes). This enables him (*a*) to handle the contact situation in an appropriately friendly way without confusion or embarrassment and (*b*) to maintain his group stereotypes relatively intact. We frequently hear the exemptor use expressions such as these: "Some of my best friends are Jews"; "That Negro minister is really a fine man—as well educated as any white minister in town."

Another common symptom of this stage of development is

the *positive overreaction* to the minority group. The person is likely to express exaggerated favorable reactions not only to the few minority members he knows but also to the whole minority group. He expresses himself in sentimental terms: "Negroes are wonderful people," or "I think the Jews are a fine people—such a rich family life!" The person fails to individualize his relationships with the group and may even adopt positive stereotypes, such as "Negroes have a wonderful ability to dance and sing," or "The Jews have such a marvelous intellectual ability!" Persons in the middle phase often believe they are completely unprejudiced and fail to realize that their overreactions imply the opposite.

A third symptom that sometimes occurs in this stage is *disillusionment* with the minority. If a person has been through a stage of idealizing the minority without really having much genuine contact with them, he is likely to expect Negroes, say, to be grateful and eager to accept persons like himself who are "so unprejudiced." He is likely to expect them to co-operate wholeheartedly in any joint project, especially if it involves improving the lot of the Negro. Frequently, patronizing attitudes creep into his interactions with minority people. When specific Negroes turn out not to be co-operative—are perhaps even a little antagonistic because they sense the patronizing attitudes—he feels rebuffed and may become unrealistic and critical. We hear such persons say that Negroes "don't appreciate what we are trying to do for them," or that they are "unco-operative" or that they "won't lift a finger unless they personally get something out of it."

3. *The mature phase.*—A person who has suffered the emotional rigors of increased intergroup activity and interaction; who has received guidance, support, and interpretation along the way; who has developed insight into his own reactions to minority-group members and their reactions to him; and who can interpret these reactions in the context of differences in background and life experience—that person then approximates

the ideal type we have called the "effective professional in intergroup relations."

Sources of Training: An Overview

Assuming that a social agency executive has eager but naïve material to work with, what are the sources of training and experience available for bringing the untrained worker to a mature point of view?

1. *Regular professional training.*—The professional social work training schools that provide group-work, casework, and community organization training, help to develop insights and skills that are essential in intergroup relations work: how to handle hostility in a professional manner, how to sense discomfort and anxiety and bring them into the open, how to introduce newcomers into group settings that may be threatening to them, how to work effectively with board members and other community people, and so on. In the long run, the better administrative jobs requiring group-work skills and community organization experience will be filled by persons holding professional degrees on the Master's and doctoral levels. Young workers looking forward to careers in intergroup relations settings should be encouraged to go on with their professional training.

2. *Ad hoc intergroup relations training.*—Occasional race relations institutes, workshops, and training courses are offered by organizations that have developed a group of experts in intergroup relations (for example, New York University teacher workshops, Fisk University race relations institutes, etc.). Although usually limited to a very few weeks, these institutes often provide an opportunity for intensive intergroup relations experiences and discussions that are valuable to the person who has had little experience in the field. Some organizations, like the YWCA, provide intensive training courses for their own new staff members that incorporate training in the skills essential to the philosophy and practices of their intergroup

relations. Young workers should be encouraged (perhaps with financial aid) to attend these training courses.

3. *Staff meetings.*—Where an active intergroup relations program is in progress, the director will probably want to devote occasional staff meetings to discussions of intergroup relations problems that arise. If a new integrated activity is being planned, if arrangements are being made to desegregate an activity previously run separately, or if some special incidents of friction occur that staff members have some doubts about having handled properly, then most staff members would benefit by frank professional discussions of the problems involved. These meetings can serve as among the best channels of communication for breaking down barriers of misunderstanding. The presence of a trained, insightful executive is essential if fruitful interchange is to be assured.

4. *Regular supervising conferences.*—It is standard practice in the more advanced social work agencies and even in some community organization groups for new and inexperienced workers to have a weekly or biweekly conference with an experienced person to appraise progress, report on assignments, and discuss the handling of new and unfamiliar situations. In these connections there are ample opportunities for interpretation of intergroup relations. Here, without the inhibiting presence of other staff members, the new worker can discuss his anxieties and discomforts with a more experienced person and receive guidance and reassurance.

5. *Interaction with staff members from other ethnic groups.*—If the agency policy is democratic and staff members of various groups are all working together in the planning and administration of program activities, instances will arise from time to time for a member of one group to explain or interpret some facet of intergroup relations to a member of another group. These may involve merely passing on factual information, or they may involve the clearing-up of misunderstandings. In

either case the relationships that grow out of them will form the basis of a more profound understanding.

6. *Working with others in the community for improved intergroup relations.*—By participating with other members of both majority and minority groups in community-wide efforts to achieve intergroup objectives, staff members can widen considerably their understanding of different points of view in intergroup relations, the reasoning and rationalizing that develop around them, and the realistic obstacles that arise to block the progress of intergroup relations.

A Specific Training Technique: The Intergroup Relations Workshop

Training in intergroup relations is most meaningful when it involves the problems and settings that practitioners face day by day. For this reason, over-all training in intergroup relations is less helpful to practitioners than separate specialized training sessions for group workers or teachers or police officers. Specially organized workshops serve this purpose well; they focus uninterrupted attention on the intergroup relations problems of a given professional group and bring the most expert talent to bear on those problems. Workshops are especially suited to intergroup relations training for group workers and recreational directors, since the workshop itself is a group-work method and group workers should be unusually successful in making the most of the opportunities that a well-designed workshop provides.

The authors have participated in a number of such workshops on intergroup relations for group workers. Several of these they helped to organize and conduct. Reflection on them suggests that a successful workshop accomplishes four major objectives for practitioners in intergroup relations.

a) A workshop is supporting to the morale of the individual practitioners who participate. In a permissive atmosphere where the practitioner can talk over the intergroup problems he is facing with others who have similar ones, he begins to understand that his problems are not unique and that others have similar anxieties about their abilities to cope with similar matters; he may find that he is doing about as well as the others in handling them. By relieving his feelings of isolation and anxiety, the practitioner will begin to develop the feeling that "we are all in this together." The group can thus be genuinely supportive to the individual worker.

b) At workshops, practitioners can begin to hammer out realistic professional standards for intergroup relations practice in their community. The unevenness of intergroup relations objectives from one organization to another can be ironed out, although it will be more difficult to arrive at uniform standards of accomplishment. The practices of the most advanced organization will perhaps become the minimum standard for all. The practitioners for whom intergroup relations was a peripheral matter will thus be encouraged to make the minimum standards for the community a central matter for their program. Where any kind of consensus is arrived at on these professional standards, they give the practitioner helpful leverage with a conservative board. He can demonstrate to his board that these intergroup objectives are standards arrived at by the profession.

c) At a workshop, the practitioner has the chance to learn specific techniques for accomplishing intergroup goals. He learns how organization A successfully handled a problem with which he is faced. From resource person B he learns of the way that the experts believe another problem he is faced with can be tackled, and so on. The workshops thus become the channels by which the best professional techniques can be circulated from one practitioner to another. Developing specific techniques and skills also helps to allay the administrative anxiety that many practitioners experience when faced with intergroup problems.

d) Workshops tend to build up helpful professional contacts and increased understanding of the resources available in intergroup relations on both the local and the national level. Resource people that serve as workshop consultants, guest speakers, panel discussants, or group leaders become known to the practitioner for the special talents and knowledge that might be helpful to him in the implementation of his program. They tend to sensitize him to the utilization of films, available pamphlets, national consultants that might be called in, and other program aids. Workshops with wide ethnic representation may provide the practitioner with meaningful personal experiences in intergroup relations. He may form contacts and friendships across group lines that will lead to a sharper perception, sensitivity, and understanding of those who are different in race, color, and creed.

The workshop is thus seen as one strategic method available to practitioners for developing greater skills and insights in handling problem situations and in exchanging experiences and thinking regarding the practice and philosophy of intergroup relations programming. When used skilfully and carefully, it becomes an important weapon in the educational arsenal of the community worker who is attempting to develop better mutual understanding among the different groups in the community.[4]

4. For a comprehensive analysis of various group methods see Herbert A. Thelen, *Dynamics of Groups at Work* (Chicago: University of Chicago Press, 1954).

CHAPTER 5

Desegregation: Changing the Practices[1]

There are few organizations with a wide range of activities that do not show some signs of segregation or "separateness." For some, it may be little more than friendship cliques and a carry-over of naturally formed neighborhood ties into organizational activities. For other agencies or groups a highly developed segregation pattern will represent the result of having, years back, set up different activity groups for majority and minority. At any rate, many officials or professional workers are faced with the problem of desegregation, and for some it will be the leading intergroup relations problem for years to come.

Segregation, Discrimination, and Prejudice

We assume that desegregation is an objective of responsible executives and boards of directors who wish to improve intergroup relations in their organizations. It is the opinion of the authors that the typical outcome of desegregation is the eventual acceptance by white persons of the participation of Negroes in certain areas of community life and in specific activities where acceptance is supported by the legitimate existing organizations and authorities, public and private. While the ease of transition from exclusion to acceptance will vary according to the nature of the particular community, the special circumstances, the level of local tension, and other such factors, the clear social fact in the United States of the 1950's is

1. Desegregation will be discussed with the Negro minority in mind, that being the group most affected by segregation in most communities. In the Far West, Indians, Mexicans, and Orientals face similar segregation. Most of the points noted would apply, regardless of the minority.

the increasing acceptance by the American public of legitimized changes in race relations. Even in those communities where there have been open resistance and hostility to these changes, only a small proportion of the white public was involved in the opposition. These individuals usually do not provide seriously disruptive and sustained opposition if they are met with firm enforcement of the new policy by responsible authorities and individuals.

Nevertheless, desegregation is blocked in many situations by persons who believe that you will inevitably have overt conflict if you bring together in mixed situations majority and minority persons who are "prejudiced" against each other.

In fact, it is widely believed that prejudice is the basic *cause* of segregation and discrimination. Many people feel that little progress can be achieved in intergroup relations until we find ways of removing the basic prejudices of individuals through some kind of educational or learning experiences. Current research suggests, on the other hand, that no such clear relationship exists between prejudice and discrimination.

PROPOSITION 6: *An important mechanism for the perpetuation of segregated situations and discriminatory practices appears to be the relatively unquestioning acceptance by people in a community of the intergroup relations practices instituted by earlier customs or policy decisions and passed along as "the way we do things here."*

An individual participating in different aspects of community life—work, neighborhood, social circle, various organizations—often will accept segregation in one area of his participation and be a stalwart proponent of equal rights in another, and yet in each situation the appropriate rationalizing attitudes and beliefs develop. We can state this as a principle:

PROPOSITION 7: *Conformity with the practices of segregation and discrimination is often quite unrelated to the intensity of prejudice in the individuals who conform.*

It is sometimes felt that the reason whites and Negroes sit in separate parts of busses in the South is that "southerners are prejudiced." But this is a half-truth. On various social-distance scales designed to measure prejudice, southerners *do* indeed express more prejudice, but this is not a sufficient cause for segregated seating on busses. A southerner who journeys to New York sits on nonsegregated busses, rides on nonsegregated subways, sits in nonsegregated theaters and baseball parks, and perhaps even eats in restaurants where Negroes are being served. He may not like these experiences, but he tends to accept them because (1) they are established practices and (2) they are accepted as appropriate by other participants. The individual prejudices of the present participants have little to do with the establishment of the practices. When in Rome, visitors generally *do* do as the Romans do.

The same is true for northerners who visit the South; they sit segregated on the busses, in the theaters, and at the baseball parks. Their individual prejudices, or lack of them, have little to do with the established practices. Furthermore, in certain border cities many northerners and southerners live in the same towns. They range all the way from highly prejudiced persons to convinced liberals. But on the northern side of the Mason-Dixon Line both prejudiced and unprejudiced sit in theaters that are mixed. On the southern side both prejudiced and unprejudiced sit in theaters that are segregated. And this is not just a matter of how close or intimate the contact is. In the South, Negroes may try on the same dresses as whites in department stores. And, of course, many southerners have close contact with servants who prepare their food, make their beds, even wet-nurse their babies. Thus the converging evidence of practical experience and our extensive research data strongly suggest:

PROPOSITION 8: *Within wide limits, prejudiced persons will accept and participate in a thoroughly mixed and integrated setting if integrated patterns are established and accepted as appropriate by other participants in that situation.*

Studies in a wide variety of American communities document this impressive fact. Where it is made quite clear by the prevailing practices that minority-group persons have the right to ride side by side with other people on the bus, shop side by side with them in the stores, work side by side with them in the factory or office, and attend schools together, then interaction in those situations is usually rapidly taken for granted as appropriate by people, regardless of their individual prejudices.

This willingness to accept different established practices, whether integrated or segregated, is illustrated by the theater patterns that existed in 1952 in two southwestern cities not many miles apart. In city A, the custom was segregated seating in the movies, with the Negroes restricted to sitting in the balconies, although whites and Negroes were mixed there. But in this same city, in the movie houses that had no balconies, Negroes were seated with whites in the orchestra. One theater owner ran two movie houses, one with a balcony and one without. So he had segregated seating in one, integrated seating in the other. Many movie-goers, with a wide range of prejudices, attended both theaters. In city B, about a hundred miles away, the movie houses also had segregated seating, and if there was no balcony, Negroes were not admitted at all. But it just happened that one theater was situated on city-owned land, and a city ordinance banning segregation in certain municipal institutions applied to it. That movie house had integrated seating. All the theaters had integrated seating for the Saturday morning children's shows. One fairly exclusive movie house in this city had no balcony. When a highly publicized movie came to that theater, a group of Negroes called the manager and indicated their desire to see it. His decision was that for the duration of the showing of that particular film Negroes would be admitted and could sit in the orchestra with the white patrons. The period of integrated seating took place without mishap. At the end of the showing of that film, the movie house reverted to its former practice of not admitting Negroes. These instances seem clearly to confirm the principle that in a wide range of situations many individuals, regardless of their individual prejudices, will go along with the operating practices that have been established and currently prevail in any particular setting as "the way we do things here."

Examination of an extensive store of research reports on organizations all over the country suggests another principle:

PROPOSITION 9: *Leaders who control the operating practices of an institution or social environment can establish intergroup policies and practices for that environment within a wide range of community customs. These new practices, even if they differ from the generally accepted prior practices, then become the established and accepted customs to which participants conform.*

What we have least understood in the past but are finding in one case after another is the wide latitude the leaders have in departing from what have been considered relatively "fixed" community mores. In a large city in the deep South, one firm had a thoroughly integrated work force in which whites and Negroes worked side by side at the same jobs for the same pay. Another firm, a fashionable restaurant, had a mixed staff in which Negroes and whites worked together in the kitchen and behind the counters, but the official statuses and roles ("counter girl," "chef's assistant," "cook," etc.) were never quite the same for whites and Negroes. Thus only the semblance of segregation was maintained, although in fact this staff was more mixed than most of the staffs of restaurants in cities with fair employment practice laws. One southwestern city had segregated schools, both on the grade- and high-school level, except for the technical high school, which was thoroughly integrated.

Yet here the junior college, which is a part of the high-school system, not only was integrated but had a Negro boy as president of its Senior class. In this same city with its segregated schools, the YWCA and the USO had integrated canteens with interracial dancing. The major determinants in these situations are not the feelings and attitudes of rank-and-file participants but the policies of the strategic persons in authority who are in positions to determine social practices.

What are the implications of these findings of our research studies for the practitioner faced with the intergroup relations problems of a given institution? First of all, they call our attention to the fact that in the historical setting where the intergroup practices for an institution evolve, key policy-setting individuals may set the patterns as either integrated or segregated, depending on how they evaluate or perceive the reaction of participants, the likelihood of friction, the criticism of peers or board members, the importance of the American creed, and similar considerations. But, once patterned as either integrated or segregated, the practices tend to be perpetuated. In many parts of the United States, these patterns often have little relationship to what other institutions in the community are doing. Once an institution realizes how relatively independent its intergroup practices are from the practices of other institutions, it becomes free of some of the fears and resistances to change that have hitherto bound it.

The question then becomes: What, specifically, are the steps that an organization with a segregated program can take to move along the road to a desegregated program?

The Importance of Policy

Assuming that there are no direct bars to desegregation, the practitioner and his board of directors can take steps to establish a policy covering desegregated activities. It is of decided advantage to practitioners to have a definite written policy statement on desegregation on the books. Some people feel that such written statements are nothing more than nice words that salve the collective conscience; and often this is the case, especially if the officers and staff do not feel strongly about implementing the policy. But if a staff is devoted to bettering intergroup relations, then a firm policy gives it a leverage point for prying away at existing practices that do not measure up to the policy—just as the Bill of Rights gives civil-rights groups a leverage point for legal action against violators. Without the Bill of Rights, their task would be much more difficult.

Some organizations, however, do not believe in setting up any interracial policy for their organizations. Thus the director of one organization states: "We do not consciously promote interracial policies. . . . We do not talk about it, and we let leadership and program follow their natural course."

Another agency in the Northeast claims that the existence of an interracial policy implies limitations of services. In support of this point of view, the director states:

We do not know how to write an interracial policy that would guarantee to Negro people the full and free use of our building. . . . Both our board and committee wrote into our discussions and records the one policy and practice—*that people are just people.* The best method (it seems to us) eliminates emphasis on, reference to, and provision for approach to people on the basis of race, creed, or religion.

A third organization expresses the same point of view in slightly different phrases:

This agency proceeds to implement its interracial policy and practice by treating all members alike. It follows the practice of not thinking of interracial practices as such, but of thinking and working for membership policies and practices for all. *We have no interracial policy.* We operate on the basis that *people are people, members are members,* and we avoid any method of interpretation which sets off one group apart from another by undue emphasis.

This point of view—that the best intergroup policy is *no* policy—deserves some thought, since it is so widely held. Undoubtedly the idea underlying it is good: that we accept on their merits all kinds of people regardless of race, creed, or origin. But it has a serious flaw. It does not set the stage for a positive implementation of desegregation and integration. By encouraging the staff to ignore "race," it virtually requires the absence of organizational machinery or conscious effort to guarantee desegregation, participation by minorities, and implementation of American Creed values. Instead, it rests its main hope for achieving these things on "the natural course of events." We have evidence from hundreds of settlement houses and recreational centers that a fully integrated intergroup relations program does not arrive in the natural course of events; where it does exist (or, more correctly, where it is approximated), it is the result of conscious, thoughtful, and painstaking work by persons with many years of experience.

In sharp contrast to the no-policy point of view is the written policy statement that explicitly provides procedures and imperatives for the establishment of an integrated program. Here is the interracial policy of a YWCA located in a southern city:

1. Since the Purpose adopted by the convention and tested by Association experience through the years stands as the one statement of faith and resolve to which all Associations are committed, that the Purpose be used as a measuring rod for policies and practices to the end that only those may be adopted or maintained which contribute to the Christian and democratic inclusiveness of the Association.
2. That the interracial practices and policies of all groups be reviewed periodically in the light of the interracial implications of the Purpose to the end that interracial policy may be *developed consistently* for the total Association and practices maintained in line with that policy.
3. That interclub council processes and other interclub activities be consciously employed to bridge the gap between groups separated by race but otherwise organized on similar bases.
4. That since national projects and conferences for constituency groups have proved useful and effective in building an inclusive movement, local Associations recognize this value, both at the point of encouraging the participation of the constituency in them and of providing opportunities for volunteers to work with these groups

to increase their acquaintance with the interracial elements of such occasions so that the impetus toward inclusiveness gained from them by the constituency may be soundly forwarded.

5-A. That, in selecting all professional staff members, candidates subscribe to the YWCA Purpose; that the interracial experience and attitudes of the candidates be carefully surveyed and evaluated in terms of the ongoing interracial development of the local YWCA and community; that candidates be willing to accord the same respect to the Negro staff members as to white; that the interracial aspects of the local situation be clearly stated in the job description; and that the responsibilities to be carried by the staff member for developing interracial understanding or activities be clearly defined.

5-B. That, in recruiting clerical and maintenance workers, the interracial character of the YWCA be clearly described and explained to all candidates; and that those be employed who are willing to work with members of the Negro race.

6. That no discrimination in salaries be made on account of race, creed or nationality; that is, that salaries be equal for equal ability, equal training and equal work.

7. That the Association evaluate its practices against the measuring rod of the Purpose as well as against the background of community mores; and that we give greater recognition *to constructive forces at work in race relations and ally ourselves with such forces.*

A policy like this strengthens the hands of organization staffs in working toward constructive changes in intergroup relations in the community setting.

Staff members in an organization that has had no intergroup policy or has had a vacillating or negative one have to develop a positive one by working with the leaders that set the policy for the organization, usually a board of directors to whom they are responsible. Their main leverage points for working with the board to develop a good intergroup policy lie in (*a*) the widespread acceptance of the moral rightness of the American Creed; (*b*) the expressed policy of the national bodies of the organization (if so affiliated); (*c*) those board members who are already in favor of integration; and (*d*) demonstrations of successful integration in one's own organization and in other organizations.

When the agency is affiliated with a national body such as

the YWCA, the Federation of Settlements, or the Boy Scouts, one effective procedure is to accept the national policy as given and interpret to the local agency board the steps being taken to implement this policy. For example:

Mr. Smith came to the border-north town of Riverton as scout executive in 1948. For the first year, he just observed what was going on about him. He saw that the Negro boys went to camp only one week out of the two-month camping period. Although this week was called "interracial week," it was obviously almost entirely a Negro affair, since the vast majority of the white boys went to camp during the earlier part of the summer. Mr. Smith was aware of the segregated nature of this procedure, but waited until his position was more firmly established before he took action.

After sounding out a few people, Mr. Smith designed the promotional literature for the 1949 summer camp. He had a few proof sheets made up which he showed to one of the board members, mentioning the fact that there was no reference to the "interracial" week at camp. When Mr. Smith showed the proof around the table at an executive board meeting, this same board member asked casually, "Where does it tell about Interracial Week?" Proceeding from this cue, Smith went on to say that he knew of no such week, that as he understood it from the constitution of the Boy Scouts of America, scouting was for all boys; and that it seemed to him that the "interracial-week" procedure implied a policy of segregation, in which neither he nor the national organization could concur. The other board members raised no objections. They went along with his decision, saying that it was all right if that was the way he wanted to run the camp; that it was, after all, his job to try to implement Boy Scout policy as best he could. There was no need to take a vote on the issue; it was considered more a change of bad practice than a change in policy. Since this policy was established, there have been Negro campers at almost every weekly period.

When the agency is a public agency, such as a city recreation board, a policy of nonsegregation can be legitimately established on the grounds that all taxpayers have a right to equal use of the facilities.

Perhaps the most difficult situation is one in which a local organization with neither public nor national affiliations has no policy on intergroup relations and has timid and vacillating practices. Here the firm establishment of a policy will aid immeasurably in achieving desegregation.

Procedures for Policy-making

In terms of strategy, some professionals feel that it is often better just to go ahead and desegregate a previously segregated activity and then confront the leaders with an accomplished fact. This procedure has a serious limitation: it may backfire and set the program back many months, as the following example illustrates:

Although nearly 20 per cent of the people in one border-north city are Negro, the YMCA program until a few years ago was all white. As a first step in correcting this situation, the Y board appointed a Negro staff worker "to help develop the Negro program." When a group of Negro boys asked this worker if they could join the learn-to-swim class, he spoke to the Y director. Together they arranged for a few handpicked Negro boys to join the group, with the joint understanding that nothing be said to the board about it. Their strategy was to present the issue as a *fait accompli*, rather than run the risk of arousing resistance by sounding out board members in advance. But the board found out by accident and proceeded to freeze desegregation efforts at the status quo, by insisting *in writing* that all further steps of this sort must be matters for board action exclusively.

The backfire effect in this instance was great. The director and Negro worker received, for their pains, (1) considerable board ill will; (2) a written policy that froze segregated intergroup relations practices and deprived the director of much personal leeway in introducing change; and (3) an eventual decision by the board to solve the "Negro problem" by setting up a *separate Negro branch*. Not until much later was any progress toward desegregation made, and this at the behest of an influential outside organization that succeeded in bringing about desegregation of the YMCA summer camps.

We feel that it is desirable to work with existing board and community leaders to establish policy, and then to desegregate under this policy. But this does not mean just initiating discussions on this controversial issue and letting the chips fall where they may. It means preparing for the discussion so that the outcome may be positive. The danger of failure to establish a progressive policy should be a warning to proceed with caution. Unorganized discussions of intergroup relations policy always run the risk of mobilizing articulate resistance.

If a policy discussion is undertaken, the agency worker usually has one basic thing in his favor: a general acceptance of the moral rightness of the American Creed. Because of the moral invulnerability of "fair play" and "equality," articulate resistance must usually skirt the issue and raise objections such as "We aren't ready for this yet," or "The minority prefers its own program," or "We can't move too rapidly in these things," or "We'll just be making a problem out of something that is going along nicely now." Because of this, it is probably better to discuss policy without reference to specific controversial situations that might arise if desegregation is undertaken. Early discussion of specifics precipitates arguments about what might happen in particular instances (like desegregating the swimming pool) and evades the issue of what the organization's broad policy ought to be. It is much better, if possible, to get board agreement to a general statement such as "If we are going to have a really democratic agency, our agency should serve *all* the people." This statement can then serve as the policy basis for later desegregation of the pool and other activities.

It may be that some board members have given little attention to racial and religious considerations as they affect agency work. These members may really have no explicit position on intergroup policy. They can be aided in forming opinions of their own by discussion with fellow board members and others who have knowledge of the considerations involved in desegregation. The board members who favor desegregation probably can be most helpful by assuming that other members will eventually favor it, for ethical or other reasons, and then helping them to participate in the implementation of this policy.

Even if the worker is not operating under a firm policy in favor of fully desegregated activities in all aspects of the program, it is helpful to have on the record a policy favoring desegregation as a goal and expressing the desirability of moving in this direction as rapidly as is feasible in the light of local conditions. Even this mild policy frees the hands of the executive of the organization to integrate as rapidly as is feasible—and he may know from experience that desegregation is feasible for many activities that his board may have great trepidation about.

One caution about procedure: In trying to establish a progressive intergroup policy, the executive may face the risks of a direct argument with his board. A direct disagreement puts him in a most difficult position. If he wins the board members over, they may be half-hopeful that he will fail and thus vindicate their position. At the first sign of trouble they can say, "We told you so," and retreat to a policy of segregation. And it puts the director in a position of trying to establish policy, which is clearly a board function. The director should remain in the role of a resource person and an agent to carry out board policy. He should be "on tap," not "on top," as an old phrase in English civil service has it.

One way to prepare for a discussion of policy for a board meeting is to confer individually beforehand with each board member who is likely to support a firm policy of desegregation. These conferences can serve to sound out such board members' reactions and their perceptions of how other members will react. Agreement can be reached as to who should bring the matter up for discussion at the board meeting (it should not be the executive), how it should be broached, who is likely to offer the major resistance, and how this may be handled, etc. These board members might agree that the executive should be asked as a resource person to comment on the practices of other agencies that have successfully desegregated or give his appraisal of the feasibility of desegregating if the board should decide it was desirable.

Policy discussions like these are best undertaken in an atmosphere that makes it possible to focus on the desirability of setting the desegregation policy clearly on the record, so that the staff and participants may know that policy without uncertainty.

Strategy for Desegregation

a) Leadership Commitment

Assuming that the practitioner now finds that he has a clear policy in favor of nonsegregation, how does he proceed? In large part the answer hinges on whether the desegregation will involve (1) a quick changeover of separate institutions or facilities, (2) a gradual desegregation of separate programs just starting, with a few activities where desegregation appears most feasible, or (3) the introduction of Negro participants into what has formerly been an all-white or predominantly white program, or vice versa. We will discuss some of the problems peculiar to each of these situations, but first a few general principles may be noted that apply to all.

PROPOSITION 10: *Desegregation that proceeds by firm and decisive steps backed by the responsible authorities is more readily accepted and taken for granted than a halting desegregation that appears unsure of itself.*

When the executive or staff members who are to administer the desegregated program are hesitant, vacillating, or doubtful about putting the nonsegregation policy into effect, they are inviting unnecessary difficulties. Weak attitudes and indecisive action in implementing desegregation tend to give encouragement to persons opposed to it and to plant doubts in the minds of other persons who are not sure just how they feel about non-segregation. Firmness and reasoned resolution, on the other hand, encourage participants to accept the new order as inevitable and to take it for granted as just another of the rules and regulations that guide the organization's day-to-day activities. This does not mean, of course, that one should be rigid and inflexible in the way one proceeds to desegregate.

It follows that a staff that is committed to nonsegregation is more likely to be successful than a staff that is not. If the staff believes wholeheartedly in improving intergroup relations by encouraging integrated activities, this is, of course, ideal. But commitment need not be construed in this all-out sense. Staffs that have had no experience with an integrated program probably hold some misconceptions about minority groups and may even doubt their ability to behave in an unprejudiced way in new interactive situations. What the executive mainly needs is an understanding by staff members that their personal feelings or prejudices have no place in their professional behavior and that they will make every effort to be sensitively impartial in trying to put nonsegregation into effect.

Securing commitment from the staff might occur through such an initial process as this: A staff meeting may be called, in which the executive makes clear the policy of the organization. He explains that he expects each staff member to give wholehearted co-operation in seeing that this policy is implemented in practice and that anyone who finds co-operation difficult should come and discuss it with him. He might explain that various staff members may have some problems as to how desegregation might be most successfully carried out in the activities they are most closely associated with and that some of these problems may require staff discussion. The important thing is this: the policy should be firmly laid down, the staff committed to it, and the problems it raises frankly discussed.

The staff usually profits from discussion of recurrent situations that they find difficult to handle. For example, one executive prepared his staff on how to answer certain recurring questions:

We coached our people on what to say to the question "Do you serve niggers here?" The answer was to be something like this, "No, we don't have any niggers. We have accepted colored people as members who are the sort that normally would want to join a Christian association. We serve them as anyone else. This is a Christian institution." This wasn't a stereotyped answer. Each person could word it in his own way.[2]

2. Shelby M. Harrison and Committee, *The Racial Factor in Y.M.C.A.'s* (New York: Association Press, 1946), p. 79.

Occasionally a staff member will balk at something expected of him under the new policy and threaten to resign if there is insistence that he comply. Usually an understanding but firm handling of the situation will dissipate such resistance. For example:

The cafeteria manager came to me and said he couldn't serve Negroes. I talked this over with one of our big industrialist board members. The board member personally had been rather neutral in our meeting, though attentive and fair. Officially he had gone along, insisting that Negroes should be served. He said, "Crack the whip on the cafeteria manager." We let the manager know that the matter of serving Negroes or not doing so was *not* in his hands. He was our employee and was earning a good salary. He was given his choice. He stayed with us, and Negroes were served.[3]

In instances like this the executive need not, of course, "crack the whip" quite so literally as this implies. He might say something like this:

I understand how you feel, but this is to be our policy, and we can't make exceptions in your case. Why don't you try it for a while? Then if you still feel the same way, let's talk it over personally to see if we can understand why you feel this way. The professionally competent worker is expected to carry out agency policy without allowing his personal feelings to interfere.

Sometimes a certain amount of ingenuity in handling a situation will bring a reluctant staff member around. One executive handled resistance to an aspect of swimming-pool desegregation in this way:

Then we got together, the locker room staff and the desk staff; the employed personnel had to be talked with. Some of them had been here for years. I had to explain everything to them. I had a harder time with them than with the board. We had about three Negro members at first. One of our oldest men, in charge of the locker room, said nothing in objection at first, but later came to me. He had been asked by one of the prominent businessmen whom he admired a lot if he was going to handle the towels and gym clothes of Negro members. The slur implied by the question had set him to thinking. He had decided that he couldn't go that far and told me so. I said he could leave the baskets of gym things belonging to any

3. *Ibid.*, p. 79.

Negro members, and as I came by each morning, I'd handle them. I meant it. That's the last I ever heard of the matter. I never found any basket to empty into the laundry.[4]

Although the desegregation policy should be made clear and explicit to staff and key leadership, no public display should be made of it by broadcasting "how democratic we are going to be"; this tends to invite comment from the persons who definitely do not approve of desegregation, and they may influence others to disapprove. Many people who have not developed a fixed set of ideas and feelings about intergroup relations can be brought to take either a favorable or an unfavorable position, depending on the social influences they face at the time.

b) Convincing the Parents

If an individual parent objects to desegregation in a program involving children, it is a good plan to invite him to the agency to talk it over. There, away from home and in an atmosphere favorable to integration, parent and executive may more calmly discuss agency policy and practice and the reasons for them. The parent can tour the agency and observe how integration works when given a chance.

Sometimes a parent will threaten to withdraw a child from participation if activities are going to be desegregated. If the executive or the staff is unable to convince the parent of the desirability of integration, they may at least be able to convince him that a decision to withdraw or not should be the child's own, after a trial period under the desegregation policy.

Dorothy Height suggests that it is a good plan to get some parents sufficiently close to the program that they can be the interpreters of it. She feels that such parents are far better interpreters than staff members, so far as other parents are concerned. She cites this instance:

4. *Ibid.*, p. 67.

In one community the camp staff worked with a group of parents on the interpretation of camp. The Camp Committee members got other parents who were sending their daughters to camp to help. Each parent was assigned time at the YWCA building and, as complaining fathers or mothers called to protest the interracial policy of the camp, the "convinced parents" talked with them. When they could say, "I'm sending Mary because . . ." a lot of good was done. The community grew in its acceptance of the interracial experience at a camp which had long held an exclusive policy.[5]

For the most part, fears of decreased participation of whites because of desegregation are exaggerated. If the atmosphere is favorable, most activities can be integrated without losing participation. When a serious loss occurs, either the setting or the situation has not been adequately appraised. Like most things, integration thrives on success, not failures. A few halfhearted tries at desegregation that fail may convince the director, board, or staff that it cannot succeed and thus choke further efforts to integrate.

c) Group Differences in Acceptance of Desegregation

Everyone realizes that some types of activities and groups can be more easily desegregated than others, but it is not easy to diagnose just how much resistance will develop in a given instance. Let us run down the list of factors that appear to be related to resistance:

1. Desegregation is generally more readily accepted in newly formed groups for which there are no clear precedents. For example, an integrated joint planning council representing all activity groups in both an all-white YWCA and its Negro branch has been found possible even in southern communities where segregation is the predominant pattern.

2. Desegregation is generally more readily accepted among younger groups. Teen-age groups, if they are coeducational and social, are among the strongest resisters of integration un-

5. Dorothy Height, *Step by Step with Interracial Groups* (New York: Woman's Press, 1946), p. 45.

less the members have grown up together as an integrated group.

3. "Natural friendship" groups are more likely to resist desegregation than "formed" or "activity" groups.

4. Groups in which membership is open will resist desegregation less than groups in which membership and participation are controlled by members themselves and therefore relatively closed to newcomers.

5. When groups are formed by staff assignment (as for places on teams), desegregation will generally meet with little or no resistance.

6. One-sex groups generally resist desegregation less than groups containing both sexes.

7. Groups oriented to special activities—such as arts and crafts, sports, and field trips—generally accept desegregation more readily than club-oriented groups formed for general companionship.

8. A favorable orientation toward American Creed values will generally reduce resistance to desegregation.

9. The more members are negatively influenced by groups outside the organization, the more difficult desegregation will be; thus camps or out-of-town conferences, where members are removed from contact with other groups that affect them negatively, provide favorable circumstances for initiating desegregation.

10. Individuals supported by and identified with a group that is amenable to desegregation will tend to go along with the group, even though they were initially inclined by background or previous experience to object. Research suggests that it is often easier to change the attitudes of a group than of an individual outside the group setting. It should be remembered that this can operate as a double-edged sword: groups can also be influenced to obstruct a desegregation program and can do so much more effectively than an individual can.

11. Neighborhood friendship groups that have their origin in a homogeneous area are likely to be resistant to desegregation.

Somehow the practitioner must weigh all these factors in the balance and determine whether a given group or activity is ready for desegregation. The key to that diagnosis is the question: Will *organized* opposition to the desegregation develop?

PROPOSITION 11: *In planning for desegregation it is important to diagnose (1) the likelihood of organized opposition developing and (2) the specific capabilities of the staff or proper authorities to dissipate any organized opposition that does develop.*

In most cases of desegregation, there are some dissident rumblings and maybe an outspoken protest or two. These individual and sporadic objections wither away as the new patterns become established and accepted. But when a few individuals begin mobilizing other people, perhaps working through established organizational channels, then this opposition must be taken seriously.

If the executive and staff foresee this kind of organized resistance, then they are faced with a difficult choice. They may try to sound out and develop support within the resistance group, at the risk of alerting the opposition and calling forth advance negative reactions (and we know that an advance sounding-out of attitudes gives a much exaggerated picture of the resistance that will actually take place). On the other hand, they may go ahead to desegregate and be ready to deal with the resistance that does develop.

d) Moving from Segregation by Policy

Among the more difficult settings in which to accomplish desegregation is that in which fairly complete separate facilities and physical plants have been provided for the two segregated groups. This situation is aggravated if the white facilities are in a white neighborhood and the Negro facilities are in a Negro neighborhood.

PROPOSITION 12: *Establishing "separate but equal" facilities may mean in the short run that more facilities will be available to Negroes, but it usually also means establishing institutional barriers that will become a major long-run obstacle to desegregation.*

For this reason every effort should be made to avoid establishing separate facilities initially. Having fewer facilities available to Negro youth for a short time is a sacrifice often worth making to avoid the obstacles arising out of a segregated setup: duplicate facilities, parallel jobs (with the development of vested interests), the establishment of segregation precedents, and the perpetuation of members' inexperience in interaction across group lines. These obstacles make a cogent argument for beginning at the outset with a joint plant and facilities.

Even in the deep South, the necessity for separate facilities may be questioned. Here is how the director of a Texas YWCA was proceeding:

In the first place, we do not have a branch YWCA in this community; therefore, any work or program must be done through our association as it recognizes the need. We have a staff and board of directors who are committed to the purpose of the YWCA. Because of this, we have attempted in the past and will continue in the future to make our program as integrated as we can, realizing, of course, that we are guided for the most part by the community mores.

Some of the steps that we have made are: (1) interracial Young Adult Conference last fall; (2) integration in some few of our association committees; (3) an interracial "hanging of the greens" party last Christmas; (4) proposed plans by the Teen-Age Department for a city-wide May Day festival of Y-Teens (Negroes and whites).

As you can see, we are slowly working out our purpose throughout our program. It will take time to become entirely integrated, but we feel that every step made is a step gained.

But assuming that separate facilities are an established fact— whether as two branches of the same organization or as two separate organizations, one serving whites, the other serving Negroes—what can be done in this situation? An appropriate first step is to bring together for planning and consultation the executives of both groups, the board members and the corresponding committees, the staff and activity leaders, and as many other parallel groups as possible for which there is an appropriate functional reason for getting together. The more situations of this sort that can be found, the easier desegregation will be in the long run. Experiences in many southern communities indicate that this is feasible and possible. Here, for example, is a communication from the director of a YWCA in a Texas city:

Our city has a Negro branch and a white branch and a Latin-American center. The white downtown branch has no program with Negroes except as the branch participates in a city-wide program with all three branches. The three branches participate together in annual meetings, and World Fellowship; and we have had a joint Teen-Age Council meeting. The YWCA is the only place in the city that will serve a meal to an interracial group. All of the metropolitan committees are interracial. In the last eight or nine years the community has become accustomed to Negroes coming into this building.

In a Tennessee city we find similar efforts to arrange interracial activities:

There is one YWCA in the city with one board of directors which is elected by all electors of the organization, regardless of race. This board of directors has as a full-fledged member the chairman of the Negro branch, who is elected by the Negro section of the YWCA membership. The Negro branch has a setup with a small governing committee. A few committees of the YWCA are interracial, such as World Fellowship and Program Planning. Other committees working in two sections come together to thrash out common problems and joint projects. The Electors' Assembly, composed of all electors, meets once a year, sometimes at the Central Branch and sometimes at the Negro branch. There are no integrated clubs; however, the Young Adult Interclub Council is interracial. There are several organizations in the city which are interracial and which meet for food at the YWCA.

The practitioner should also consider the possibility of using "extra-community" events as a steppingstone to desegregation. National and regional conferences that are planned on a non-segregated basis often provide participants with their first experiences in integrated living. Overnight journeys or extended camping trips provide similar opportunities. These "living-to-gether" experiences have special advantages: (a) they are likely to be emotionally satisfying and interesting and therefore tend to have reinforced meaning to participants; (b) they provide continuous interaction among the segregated groups over an extended period; (c) the inhibiting influences of family and community are temporarily absent; (d) there are many opportunities for fairly intimate contact; (e) the newness of the situation permits great administrative flexibility in assigning mixed groups.

These living-together experiences are more fruitful preparations for desegregation if they are followed up in the year-round program of the organization. For example, one might use the friendships established during the living-together experiences as the core of a joint planning committee to discuss what other program activities might be held jointly by the white and Negro organizations. With a little imagination, officers and staff of segregated organizations who want to widen the intergroup experiences of their members can find many situations where nonsegregated activities would be appropriate—e.g., an athletic council to plan sports competitions among the various organizations, an exhibition committee to plan a joint show of the arts-and-crafts activities of different organizations, a Brotherhood Week committee to plan a human relations program, and so on. Sometimes these joint committees can form the basis for new nonsegregated activities where integration is unprecedented. For example, in a community where sports have been segregated, an athletic council may arrange that, at the end of a season of competition among the teams from various organizations, an all-star team be designated. The chances are good that the all-star team would be mixed, white and

Negro, if the athletes were picked strictly in accordance with ability. Then perhaps the next year arrangements could be made for the all-star team to play the all-star team of a neighboring community.

If the nonsegregated all-star team is accepted (and we think it usually would be), then perhaps the following year participation in sports could be widened to include a greater age range, with players assigned to teams in accordance with age or ability so that only teams of similar caliber would play each other. Color would be ignored, and the teams would be mostly mixed, if ability alone is the criterion of assignment.

Where there are separate organizations for whites and Negroes and the jointly planned activities have been fully exploited, a likely next step is desegregation by the elimination of duplicate facilities and staff leadership functions. For example, suppose that both a white and a Negro settlement house have a model-airplane hobby group. The white group use as leader a volunteer who is leaving town. The Negro group leader is the local shop teacher from the Negro school who has extensive experience with model planes and is obviously the best-qualified leader in town for such a group. Instead of feverishly hunting around for a white leader, the joint planning council could recommend that white boys interested in model airplanes enrol in the group run by the Negro shop teacher. It would then be possible for the white organization to concentrate on providing leadership and facilities (perhaps space released by no longer running a model-airplane group) for some other activity, which in turn might be made available to Negroes. By this type of division of labor and specialization, the most could be made of both physical plants as desegregation proceeded, and both groups would benefit from the elimination of duplicate facilities.

One steppingstone to the joint use of facilities is the initial use of a facility that only one organization has—say, a swimming pool—on a segregated basis. Negroes might have been scheduled to use the pool at certain times during the week. Building on this situation, a joint committee could be set up to draw up rules and regulations on safety, use of lockers or baskets, etc. Then when school starts (or stops), the committee could discuss the scheduling of times for white and Negro use. Out of such discussion may come a plan for total desegregation of the pool.

PROPOSITION 13: *Desegregation is sometimes brought about by establishing joint planning committees and providing procedures by which the decision to desegregate can be arrived at by the joint committee itself.*

Where the problem is to desegregate activities that are firmly established as segregated, ingenuity and imagination will be required to devise situations and procedures that will lead the groups toward desegregation. But one thing is becoming increasingly clear: new and unprecedented situations, activities, or groups need not follow segregated patterns just because segregation has been the prevailing way of handling intergroup relations in the past. The Cornell research group, conducting community studies focused on intergroup relations, needed both white and Negro interviewers for a survey in Savannah, Georgia. It was efficient to train the interviewers in two groups, and interviewers were assigned to the time most convenient for them, regardless of color. Since this was obviously a practical arrangement and one for which no existing patterns of segregation prevailed, it was accepted without objection. Wherever segregated groups are under one administrative control, similar possibilities are present.

e) Moving from Exclusion in Practice

Many northern communities are faced with a somewhat different problem in desegregation. The policy of an organization may be quite explicit in permitting whites and Negroes to participate together in the activities, but for one reason or another most or all of the activities are all-white. What can be done in this instance? There are several possibilities.

1. The organization can make its physical facilities available to groups or organizations that have an intercultural philosophy. There may be times when youth groups of the National Association for the Advancement of Colored People, Urban Leagues, International Clubs, or foreign-student groups from local educational institutions would have reason to make use of meeting-rooms, cafeterias, the gymnasium, or some other available facility. The presence of these groups will set the intergroup atmosphere of the agency, demonstrate organization policy to members and other visitors, help to allay minority persons' doubts as to whether they are really wanted, and may even provide new recruits for the organization's own activities.

2. The organization can accept all-minority groups as a starting point for initiating intergroup experiences and paving the way for more complete integration. Sometimes, perhaps because of residential segregation or other mutual experiences, friendship groups of children or teen-agers will be homogeneous (all Negro, all Mexican, all white, etc.). If they know that an organization's facilities are available, they may want to affiliate as a club, with their composition intact. This would mean a segregated group. Some professional workers tend to reject the all-Negro club because they feel it is contrary to a policy of nonsegregation, but this is a rather rigid and mechanical way to think about the problem.

An all-Negro club of this sort is often just as "natural" as other friendship clubs that are mixed and should not have to break up as the price of admission to the agency program. Under skilled leadership, members of the all-Negro group will become involved in club council activities, athletics, and organization-wide events, where they will interact and become friends with persons of other races and national backgrounds. Over a period of time the composition of the group can change to include members of other groups. In time the group itself may be replaced by other groups oriented toward interests that cut across ethnic lines. It takes considerable time for members of a group that is tightly knit to expand their contacts and grow in confidence and experience to the point where they can assimilate intergroup experiences that formerly were threatening. Under guidance, such a group can move steadily along toward the intergroup relations philosophy of the organization, but only if the group is accepted into the program as a starting point. An example of a rigid "no-segregation" policy that resulted in increased segregation is the following:

A small Indian population lives scattered through one southwestern city, and a large number of Indians live on reservations surrounding the city. Because they felt that the Indians needed a recreation center, a minister from the local Bible school and an Indian who had been trained there asked the YMCA for space in its new building for this purpose. They asked for a separate room to be set aside as an "Indian room," since they felt that, at least at first, the Indians would be shy about mingling with whites. The YMCA executive refused this request on the grounds that Y policy prohibited segregation of any group. Indians, he said, were free to join the YMCA as individuals, but not as an all-Indian group.

As a result of this refusal, there are no Indians in the YMCA, either as individuals or in groups. The Indian center that was subsequently established with the help of a national religious organization is one dingy basement room with poor plumbing and almost no facilities. Nevertheless, it is frequently crowded to overflowing by Indian families that go there. It is developing a reputation throughout the Indian people of Arizona, and its director is able to perform many social services for Indian families that need counseling or other help. In this case the YMCA passed up an opportunity to help in the social integration of what is probably the most physically and culturally isolated minority group in the Southwest.

There is a danger that natural friendship groups of one racial or nationality background may continue as homogeneous groups and participate in the organization's program in a limited way. In fact, agencies that may have some hesitation in adopting a thoroughly integrated program might encourage the participation of homogeneous friendship groups with the idea of perpetuating segregation and isolation. This would be unfortunate. These natural groupings should be permitted to participate only with the understanding that their being a part of the organization is a first step to widening the intercultural experiences of their members.

TABLE 6

EXECUTIVES OF AGENCIES THAT HAVE ONE OR MORE SOCIAL WORK TRAINED WORKERS ON THEIR STAFFS AND ARE JUDGED EFFECTIVE DIFFER FROM EXECUTIVES OF OTHER AGENCIES IN THEIR ATTITUDES TOWARD DIFFERENT ACTION EFFORTS

	Trained Worker on Staff and Judged More Effective (Per Cent)	Trained Worker on Staff and Judged Less Effective, or No Trained Worker on Staff and Judged Effective (Per Cent)	No Trained Worker on Staff and Judged Less Effective (Per Cent)
Total cases..................	33	84	116
Which do you feel *predominates* in your attitudes during your day-to-day work on the job? "We should open our doors to all groups regardless of creed or color and then build our program around the people that voluntarily show interest in our activities"........	39	49	57
"We should go out of our way to try to find inducements to get minority-group participation even if the minorities seem suspicious or reluctant to participate".............	61	51	43
	100	100	100

3. The organization can make a special effort to form new activity groups that start off as mixed groups. As Table 6 shows, the better-trained and more effective practitioners realize that frequently an effort has to be made to recruit minority participation. It is not enough merely to open the agency's doors to all. Participation must be purposefully planned and organized.

Because it appears more difficult to add Negroes or other

minority members to an existing group where the in-group ties have become firmly welded, it is often wise to delay the formation of a new group until minority participants have been recruited. This may take some spadework, but it is worth it. If minority recruits for a youth activity are wanted, two likely sources are the school and the minority organizations of both youth and adults. A visit to the local school principal is likely to bring forth names. It is wise to get the names of close companions (either minority or majority), since several together may be inclined to sample a new activity in a strange setting where one alone might be hesitant to participate, especially if he is a minority member fearful of rebuff. Also, a few words before some of the minority organizations, indicating the desire of the agency to extend its facilities to all groups in the community, will help to get the word around that the minority is welcome. Besides creating a favorable opinion of the organization in the minority community, the lines of communication that are established by this spadework may be useful in other intergroup relations work. To get actual participants in any given activity, it may be necessary to get the specific names of persons that might be interested and extend invitations to them personally.

4. Perhaps the most difficult situation to handle is the introduction of minority members into activity or friendship groups that have been in existence for some time and have formed in-group loyalties. It is easier if the group is an activity group with a generally open-membership policy. If a friendship group or club has a closed policy and the members vote on new members, resistance may develop. Actually, we know little about the best ways to handle such a situation. If the agency policy has been made explicit from the outset and demonstrated in numerous other activities, one approach is for the director to show up at a meeting with a minority recruit or two, explain that they are interested in joining a group, and ask the leaders to explain something about this group's activities. Then by carefully guiding the interaction to bring out the

naturally friendly gestures that most youngsters tend to show in such a situation, the director can probably bring about at least a tentative participation.

Some practitioners feel that if it is desirable to introduce new minority members to an ongoing cohesive group, some preparation of the group is necessary. The main danger in preparation is the likelihood of arousing the doubts and fears that anticipation of an unfamiliar experience often awakens. Advance preparation is probably more necessary, the more articulate the resistance, the more unprecedented the situation in relation to current agency practice, and the more organized the opposition.

Any preparation that is made should avoid speech-making, "moralizing," and condescension. There should be a free airing and handling of objections. Considerations of fairness, democratic beliefs, and the American Creed should be the articulated assumptions on which the group decision to "try it out" should be based. Preparation should stress the adjustments that members will be making in order not to "hurt peoples' feelings" and to make them "feel at home." If the situation has been set properly and the discussion skilfully handled, most youth groups, at least in northern settings, will probably agree to give it a try.

f) In Summary

There is no simple formula for desegregating; each situation must be diagnosed and prescribed for in keeping with its own peculiar circumstances. But there are some rules of thumb that seem valid. If we put them in oversimplified form as a tentative blueprint that might be called "How To Desegregate Your Organization," it would look something like this:

1. Announce firmly and explicitly to your staff that the board has established a policy of nonsegregation. Explain the reasons for it. Emphasize the importance of achieving an orderly transition without fanfare.

2. Enlist the commitment of your staff in achieving a fair and impartial enforcement of the new policy. Hold small meetings with your staff to make clear your expectation of co-operation. Show that you understand that there may be private feelings of prejudice among staff members, and invite anyone who feels unable to co-operate to meet with you *individually* to discuss it further.

3. Reassure your staff members that desegregation is possible; recognize and deal with their anxieties and discuss any disruptive rumors that may have gotten started. Explain that experience has shown that the widely varying prejudices of individuals need not be a serious bar to successful desegregation. Explain that individual instances of friction are to be expected, but emphasize that they offer good opportunities to make the new policies explicit, to make clear the staff's intention to be firm in the matter, and to help people to gain new understandings.

4. Wherever possible, involve members of your staff, both white and Negro, in the joint planning of new assignments and the procedural details that the change-over will involve. Where possible, get board members to help in this.

5. Anticipate the kinds of situations that might cause friction and set up procedures for handling them. It may be wise to draw up a list of the major types of objections that you are likely to receive and, *with your staff*, decide how they can best be answered. Do not let protests be taken over the head of lower-level staff members to you or to board members. Refer these protests back to the lowest level where they can be handled and back up decisions made by your staff whenever possible. If it becomes necessary to reverse a lower-level decision, do it only with and in the presence of the person who made the initial decision. Train your staff *not to argue* with protesting persons but to further explain the new policy and calmly state that no exceptions can be made. Have staff members patiently and understandingly listen to complaints, then suggest

that the protesting person try the situation for a while to "see how it works."

6. Make all assignments that may appear as differential treatment (e.g., assigning white members to a Negro staff person) on the basis of some objective criterion that can be easily defended, such as alphabetical order of names, age, height, etc.

7. Take whatever steps you can to identify any sources of organized opposition and plan ways to meet this antagonism if it should develop. Encourage the leaders of any organized opposition to come to your board to express their point of view and feelings. Perhaps ask them to work with an appropriate committee to see that their legitimate objectives are obtained (e.g., that certain physical facilities, such as the swimming pool or gym, do not become overcrowded). Beware of mass meetings with the opposition; it is extremely difficult to deal constructively with objections at large public gatherings.

8. Enlist the aid of responsible leaders among your long-term membership (both white and Negro) in organizing procedures to make the change-over as harmonious as possible. They can be invited to appoint a committee to work with the staff, assisting in desegregation.

As we have said, no one simple secret of success exists in the transition from segregated to integrated facilities. But there is, we believe, one factor that may be the single most important predictor of success or failure in achieving full desegregation and public acceptance of a desegregated program. That factor is the degree of *reasoned firmness* with which the legitimate leaders or authorities in the situation tackle the job of desegregating the organization and its program. We do not mean that the leaders should proceed rigidly, ignoring individual and group variations in readiness to change. We do mean that the more firm and explicit the leaders are in moving toward the ultimate goal, the sooner desegregation will be taken for granted as "the way we do things here."

CHAPTER 6

Integration: Establishing the Values

There is a widespread belief that when an organization has established policies and practices that are nonsegregated and has a reasonable amount of minority and majority participation, then the intergroup relations objectives have been achieved. But this is not necessarily the case. Desegregation may have been achieved, but not integration. "Integration," as we are using the term, refers to the *process of unlearning prejudices and establishing new democratic values through interaction in a nonsegregated environment.* It is a continuous process that takes place as long as new participants are being brought into the organization. It is the intergroup relations dimension of the personal growth that every group worker hopes to develop in members who participate in his program. In other words, integration is a process, as well as a goal.

The Nature of Prejudice

To understand this process of integration, we need first to explore briefly some of the principal characteristics of prejudice.

Most majority-group prejudices (at least in northern urban communities) are rather superficial negative attitudes toward, or misconceptions about, minorities. They are acquired mostly from contacts with prejudiced people rather than from contacts with minority groups themselves. They are transmitted in much the same way as are Bible stories, food preferences, or tastes for a certain type of music. These prejudices thrive on recognizable group differences such as skin color or accent. They flourish in the absence of corrective communication through contact wtih minorities. They often feed into misleading stereotypes that become the agreed-upon currency of communication.

Stereotypes are learned in the same way as table manners: by association with people who have that kind of table manners. We learn stereotypes by association with people who have these misconceptions, not necessarily by contact with the objects of the stereotypes. Because stereotypic thinking prevails in many parts of our society, most people learn it, and, in this sense, prejudice is "normal." This type of prejudice, however, may not be deeply rooted, and in many persons it yields readily to various kinds of corrective communication.

But if a person's social environment is highly ethnocentric, such that he has strong feelings of identification with his own group, then it may be difficult for corrective communication to reach him. This is often true whether he be Italian, Jewish, or New England Yankee. If this ethnocentrism is accompanied by prejudices about others and if the individual has little intergroup contact at work, at play, or in the neighborhood, then corrective communication is difficult to apply.

Although much prejudice is a matter of learning and social conformity, we must not overlook the more serious "personality-rooted" prejudice. In the so-called "authoritarian" person we find a group of personality factors that include suspiciousness and distrust of other people, a view of the world as a threatening place and of other groups as trying to get ahead at one's expense. When things go wrong, it's the other fellow's fault, and the authoritarian is ready to seize on the nearest appropriate scapegoats.

Scapegoating appears to have its roots in hostility, that continuously reactivated bitterness and hatred that some people have developed because of unfortunate emotional relationships. But since in our society one is supposed to love his fellow-men, hostility is often repressed and not acknowledged. The authoritarian may appear on the surface to be friendly, kind, and optimistic about life, but beneath this socially acceptable exterior lie repressed hostility, guilt feelings, or anxiety.

Authoritarians generally release their hostility in ways that are least threatening to their established social relationships. Hence the appeal of "scapegoats" such as Jews, Negroes, or the foreign-born. These provide objects against which antagonism can be vented, often without reprisal.

Prejudice and Behavior in Intergroup Situations

It is widely believed that the accumulation of prejudices a person acquires from his culture through his family and his peer groups determines in large measure how he will act in new intergroup situations. In part this is true. But at the same time research is providing increasing evidence for the following proposition:

PROPOSITION 14: *The newcomer to a nonsegregated social environment learns from its regular participants the appropriate forms of interaction and sentiment for that environment, and these often are even more important in regulating his behavior in that particular environment than his past experiences and current prejudices.*

Most individuals live within a fairly narrow range of social environments. Each environment bears down on the individual with its own social pressures, its own special standards of attitudes and behavior. A man who accepts quite naturally, for example, the participation of Jews in his service club or as neighbors may object strongly to having Jews belong to his golf club. Workers who accept and vote for Negroes as officers in their union may strongly oppose having a Negro family move into their neighborhood. On the other hand, we have observed cases where a white family moves into a neighborhood and finds that a "nice, respectable" Negro family is living down the block and that the other white neighbors accept the family and are even seen to be neighborly with them; the typical out-come is that the new residents rapidly come to take for granted the fact that they have a Negro neighbor. Current research findings lead increasingly to this generalization:

PROPOSITION 15: *Major changes in individual prejudices oc-cur most quickly and thoroughly from exposure to social inter-action in a new social environment rather than from informa-tion and exhortation alone.*

A newcomer to a social environment or institution where he wants to be accepted is likely to be unusually sensitive to other participants' perceptions of his behavior and to their approval and disapproval. Because of this sensitivity, the significant per-sons in an integrated situation or environment tend to become an important group in setting standards of behavior for the new participant. We tend to pattern our conduct after the conduct of those already in the particular situation.

If the social atmosphere is favorable to integration, then the normal, reasonably secure person can assimilate new interac-tive experiences without much strain. What appears to happen is this: most individuals have already developed habitual ways of handling contacts with whomever they happen to meet. When they are placed in an interactive situation with a mi-nority-group member, the same patterns tend to be called forth, since often they are the only interpersonal techniques the in-dividual has for handling interaction with anyone. This is espe-cially likely if the minority member is well trained in the social graces of the majority. Majority-group persons are often amazed to meet a member of a minority group who behaves "just like anyone else." If this behavior fails to fit in with some stereotypic conceptions of the majority-group person, he often sees the minority person as "different" from most others and exempts him from the prejudices he holds against the total group. The main point is this: we can usually depend upon the interlocking interpersonal habits of the participants in an intergroup situation to help bring about friendly relationships in that situation.

PROPOSITION 16: *Interaction in a favorable environment generally leads to friendship formation between majority- and minority-group persons, regardless of the level of disengaged prejudice in the individual.*

It is this principle that gives us confidence that integration can be most readily achieved by bringing people together in a favorable atmosphere with confidence that friendly interaction will prevail. We can then handle the tension incidents and problems of communication as they develop.

A newcomer to an integrated social environment with customs different from the environments in which he has previously participated is likely to commit slips, errors, and minor transgressions that call forth anxiety and discomfort on his own part and disapproval and criticism from the regular participants. If the negative feelings generated in these interpersonal frictions are "worked through" (i.e., resolved by interpretation, insight, and understanding), then mutual rapport tends to be generated and a positive relationship established. Misconceptions and stereotypes can be cleared up during this process of establishing relationships, and the fair-play values that underlie the integrated practices can be made articulate. Through this process, prejudices are *un*learned and the American Creed established as a conscious part of the individual's personal value system.

It follows, then, that the integration process can be successfully carried on in community settings where the general level of prejudice or the prevailing community customs may at first seem prohibitive. Out of the interactions provided in the organizational setting come many personal satisfactions but also numerous minor frictions and tensions. The clearing-up of these frictions and misunderstandings is a major process for modifying prejudices, creating intergroup friendships, and developing commitment to personal values that embody the American Creed. It is precisely in the area of handling tensions and hostile feelings that the skill and insight of the professional social group worker is needed.

The Practitioner's Role

How can the executive and staff of an organization make use of a nonsegregated environment to establish democratic values in the thinking of the persons who participate in that environment? This is the sixty-four-dollar question—one to which no glib and facile answers suggest themselves. The basic sociological process appears to be this: we work with new participants through the informal social processes of interaction, to get them to accept and believe in the norms established as the ways of behavior of the integrated setting. Just how attitudes and values are modified in these integrated settings is not clearly understood. But at several different points in the process the opportunities for social processes to work are optimal.

a) Induction

When new participants are brought into the organization, its policy on intergroup relations can be clearly enunciated in the routine course of explaining rules and regulations. The newcomer can be told that the staff expects individuals to be accepted because of their individual worth, apart from their race or religion. He can be told that the organization offers an opportunity for members to meet and get to know people of different backgrounds and experience. It might even be explained to him that talk or behavior that belittles any person because of his race, religion, or extraction is entirely out of place in this sort of democratic environment. As integration proceeds, it may be enough merely to reaffirm these sentiments and indicate an expectation of compliance. The aim is to establish a "taken-for-granted" attitude toward integration.

b) Interpretation

Opportunities sometimes arise for staff members to interpret the background or experience of one participant in the program to another. Perhaps the Christian boy doesn't realize that the Jewish boy doesn't celebrate Christmas and makes some remark that reveals his ignorance. The organization leader might explain this to him and point out that Chanukah holidays correspond in some ways to the observance of Christmas but have their own special meaning because the Jewish religion is different from the Christian religion.

Because minority-group differences are real and recognized differences, an intergroup relations worker, if he is to interpret minority behavior to others, needs himself to understand and be sympathetic to the experience of the minority person. Trained practitioners in intercultural settings have learned to see into the emotional and psychological reactions of the minority persons with whom they are dealing, especially as these reactions are conditioned by ethnic status.

The minority-group member of a settlement house or community center who engages in athletics, arts and crafts, or dancing is sometimes expected to be "outstanding" or "twice as good" by the practitioner. This is often true for Negroes participating in athletics. The stereotype that all Negroes have remarkable physical development is shared by many Americans. The practitioner may scarcely be aware of the fact that he is influenced by this stereotype; yet his behavior, especially in supervising competitive sports, may reveal that he expects the Negro participant to excel.

With Jewish participants the same situation prevails. The Jewish child learns from his elders the nature of the real world he faces and that prejudice and discrimination do really exist. He may then get the idea that to succeed in his chosen line of endeavor he will have to be twice as good as anyone else. Especially in small Jewish communities, where factory or industrial workers are rare and where the Jewish group consists primarily of middle-class families, the Jewish youngster often has ambitions in business or the professions, and unusually high performance is expected of him by teachers and others.

It would seem, then, that the social situation that faces the minority-group child puts pressure upon him through various sources to excel if he is to succeed. Practitioners dealing with minority-group members during their formative years need to be aware of this situation and handle the child with understanding of the extra strain these high standards place on him.

Sometimes practitioners who are themselves minority-group members unwittingly intensify this process by serving as the principal agents for stamping such an ideology of excellence on the thoughts and actions of minority-group children. A Negro practitioner with middle-class values, who is rising in socioeconomic status and is perhaps sensitive about his own working-class origins, may judge the Negro children too harshly in terms of his own standards of correct behavior. He may criticize even mildly inappropriate behavior, such as swearing or roughneck activity, and tell the offenders that they are discrediting the entire Negro race, whereas a white child in a similar situation receives merely a routine reprimand.

In one community, after much negotiating, the first Negro teacher was appointed to a regular position. Later, a number of Negro parents at P.T.A. meetings told white parents with some feeling that the Negro teacher was "tougher on the Negro kids than the white teachers were." It seems that the Negro teacher was eager to see every Negro student get good grades and be a well-behaved child in school. Many of the Negro children were from working-class homes, where there was less encouragement of scholastic achievement and less emphasis on middle-class manners. Many Negro parents, believing it was difficult enough for Negro children to compete in ordinary ways with white children, felt that the Negro teacher was pressing their children too strongly to adopt what were, for the time, unrealistic middle-class aspirations. In this same community, a Jewish teacher, who had a Ph.D. and had studied in Europe, was extremely well thought of. Once, when conducting a vocational-guidance course for the Jewish teen-agers at the Jewish center, she told the students: "Precisely because you are Jews, and a minority in each class, you must do better than the gentile child if you are to win respect and acceptance."

A young person, whether of minority- or majority-group status, is generally alienated by this sort of judgmental attitude. He needs to be accepted for what he is. He should not be made to feel that he must "qualify" for the professional worker's affection and respect by *changing* his behavior and his attitudes. He should be seen as the end result of many social, economic, and psychological forces. If the child curses, is aggressive, is untidy about his appearance, and generally does not conform to certain middle-class standards of behavior and conduct, it does not mean that he is "bad" and therefore not worthy of respect and attention.

Davis and Havighurst have pointed out[1] that the slum child, the child coming from a disadvantaged home or neighborhood that places a premium on aggressive behavior, may be perfectly "normal" in that his behavior and attitudes are a response to realistic environmental obstacles. It is ironic that the Negro child, already struggling against handicaps of prejudice and discrimination, is expected to *do* better, to *be* better, than the white child, if he is to gain acceptance and a place in the world. The strain is too great, and, as Kurt Lewin has observed, the minority child "tries too hard; he is overworked, too tense, and overaggressive."

What are the implications of minority experience for the intergroup practitioner? If he is to relate successfully to a minority person, the practitioner accepts him for what he is, not for what the practitioner would like him to be. He is con-

1. A. Davis and R. J. Havighurst, "Social Class and Color Differences in Child-rearing," *American Sociological Review*, XI (1946), 698–710.

tinually aware that deviant behavior has meaning, often with deep roots in family and neighborhood background and in the emotional perspectives created by bitter minority experiences. Behavior, whether aggressive or withdrawing, needs to be understood and constructively handled. It is better to steer away from judgments of "good" or "bad" in favor of understanding the meaning of such behavior. The effective practitioner tries to re-evaluate his own feelings about such things as cleanliness, politeness, and good behavior, where he finds those feelings interfering with acceptance of minority behavior. The swaggering, superficially aggressive, "Dead End kid" may have a fine potential for participation and leadership; the well-behaved, shy, and compliant person one "takes to" immediately may find it much harder genuinely to accept a person of different ethnic status. The trained practitioner tries to look beyond surface behavior to the real personality underneath.

Where members of a group have been unequal in terms of opportunity, family background, and existing discrimination, they need to be treated individually, differentially, in effect "unequally," if they are truly to be treated as equals. Minority reactions to minority status may range all the way from acute self-hatred and flight to comfortable acceptance and pride in one's own group. Effective professional workers understand the uniqueness of the different minority individuals they work with and start by accepting hostile, ingratiating, or status-striving minority behavior *as it is,* recognizing (1) that its roots lie in the life-experiences of the minority persons and (2) that it can change. Important as it is to have the long view into the past history of an individual in understanding his present reactions, it is equally important to have a long view into his future levels of development. The minority person who is a newcomer to the agency may be anxious or awkward or aggressive. If he is met with a realistic acceptance, these surface characteristics may be quite rapidly modified and replaced by a greater measure of ease and security.

c) Friction Incidents

Friction incidents are often thought to be the symptoms of a deteriorating intergroup situation, where covert tension has finally broken through into overt conflict. But in the day-to-day processes of integration, where persons with little intergroup experience are brought together in new interactive situations, "incidents" are bound to occur. They should be anticipated and handled appropriately. Viewed as the "growing pains" of adjustment to integration, they can often be used constructively to improve intergroup relationships further.

Many incidents result from bringing together majority- and minority-group persons who think in stereotypes about each other's group. In an atmosphere that encourages persons to verbalize and articulate their feelings, these misconceptions frequently emerge as slips of the tongue or barriers to communication that cause discomfort, hurt feelings, and tension. Their occurrence, however, offers a real opportunity for clarification, interpretation, and education. In this sense, "tension" is normal rather than pathological.

This point emerges clearly from some of the data from the survey of YWCA's and neighborhood houses mentioned earlier. In rating the individual executives on the effectiveness of their intergroup relations programs, a larger proportion of the executives who reported friction incidents were rated among the "more effective" (see Tables 7 and 8). Friction incidents more frequently accompanied the "good" situations where efforts were being made to integrate or desegregate than where the situation was static. There is a folk saying that "you can't make an omelette without breaking some eggs." We might also say, "You can't achieve intergroup integration without engendering some friction."

Another type of friction involves real personal antagonisms that have been channeled into interethnic expression. Some boys get into a squabble on the basketball floor, and in anger one of the white boys shouts, "Aw, you jigs never play fair!"

The perceptive practitioner tries always to distinguish and disentangle personal hostility from intergroup misunderstanding. Perhaps a rough typology will make this point clear. If we classify incidents by how much *personal* hostility is involved

TABLE 7

HOLDING TRAINING CONSTANT, EXECUTIVES OF AGENCIES WHO RE-
PORT TENSION INCIDENTS ARE MORE LIKELY THAN OTHERS
TO BE JUDGED MORE EFFECTIVE

	HAVE TRAINED WORKER ON STAFF		NO TRAINED WORKER ON STAFF	
	No Tension	Tension	No Tension	Tension
Total cases..................	33	90	88	97
Per cent judged more effective.	39	58	18	40

TABLE 8

HOLDING DEGREE OF INTEGRATION CONSTANT, EXECUTIVES OF
AGENCIES WITH TENSION INCIDENTS ARE MORE LIKELY
THAN OTHERS TO BE JUDGED MORE EFFECTIVE

	UNDER 40 PER CENT OF ACTIVITIES INTEGRATED		40–80 PER CENT OF ACTIVITIES INTEGRATED		OVER 80 PER CENT OF ACTIVITIES INTEGRATED	
	No Tension	Tension	No Tension	Tension	No Tension	Tension
Total cases........	38	40	26	82	57	65
Per cent judged more effective.........	26	35	23	56	23	48

and then subdivide them by how much *intergroup* antagonism is involved, four types can then be defined: (A) incidents involving no personal hostility *or* group antagonism (e.g., a child slips and uses the word "nigger" in counting out, "Eeny, meeny, miney, mo"); (B) incidents involving personal hostility and only secondarily intergroup differences (e.g., a child who has been bested in competition by a minority person expresses his chagrin by hurling an ethnic epithet at his rival); (C) incidents involving group antagonisms but no personal hostility (e.g., a gang of boys, sensing the negative reactions of adults to Negroes moving into the neighborhood, taunts individual Negro youngsters on their way to school); (D) incidents involving the channeling of personal hostilities into organized scapegoating (e.g., some white boys bully and beat a Negro youngster to increase their own feelings of adequacy).

	Personal Hostility Absent	Personal Hostility Present
Intergroup antagonism absent	A	B
Intergroup antagonism present	C	D

Obviously, no fixed prescriptions can be laid down for handling each of these different types of situations. Depending on what the practitioner knows about the different participants and the individual peculiarities of the situation as it develops, he will modify his handling of friction incidents from one instance to the next. But a few general principles should probably be borne in mind in deciding on an appropriate course of action.

It is generally unwise to let a friction incident pass without doing something about it at the time. Letting a slip or an epithet pass without picking it up may give a misleading impression to a minority participant, other minority spectators, and the other spectators who witnessed the incident. Besides, the offender himself may perpetuate his impression that the offending behavior is not taboo. Just as in the case of disciplining a child, the best time to handle an intergroup situation that needs action is when it comes up. There may be aspects that will need additional treatment later, but incidents should not be passed over entirely at the time they occur on the grounds that they can be better handled privately later. An important thing about a favorable intergroup relations atmosphere is that it is not private. A good atmosphere requires public recognition, and the opportunities that friction incidents provide to reaffirm the prevailing policy and practices should not be missed.

PROPOSITION 17: *A person can more easily accept criticism of objectionable intergroup behavior if he is helped to understand that the criticism is not a rejection of himself as a person.*

The practitioner in handling incidents in which participants express intergroup antagonisms or prejudices should try to make clear that he is objecting to specific behavior and not disapproving of the persons who manifested that behavior. A practitioner who overreacts with hasty, impulsive, judgmental behavior is behaving unprofessionally and may damage his relationship with the offending member. This will weaken his leverage for improving the intergroup relations reactions of the offender and his peers. After all, the relationships that the practitioner establishes with participants in his program are the main avenues of therapeutic movement he has available to him. The skill with which he handles these relationships is a measure of his technique as a practitioner. Anything that impairs those relationships jeopardizes his program. This is why an understanding of minority experience by the practitioner often leads the minority participants in the program to gain confidence in him.

A corollary of the foregoing point is this: The practitioner should try not to embarrass a person in the eyes of his peers. It is especially demoralizing to be shown up before one's friends. Besides risking impairment of the relationship with the practitioner, the whole group may become unified in opposition to him if one of them, especially a leader, is reprimanded. Cohesive cliques, where the strong in-group and out-group feelings become focused on ethnic differences, represent a real threat to a successful intergroup relations program.

PROPOSITION 18: *Objectionable behavior should be publicly challenged, with an explanation of why it is not acceptable; but the practitioner should arrange to hold individual interview sessions where the offender's personal feelings can be appropriately discussed.*

How much of an incident is handled publicly or privately depends on which of the various types of friction a given incident is diagnosed to be. Obviously, type A incidents (both personal and intergroup hostility absent) can generally be handled routinely as they come up. For example, if a child says, "Eeny, meeny, miney, mo, catch a nigger by the toe," the practitioner can just stop him and say, "We don't use that word around here—it's not a nice word. Use the word 'tiger' instead—'catch a *tiger* by the toe.' OK?"

Type C incidents (personal hostility absent, intergroup antagonism present), also could probably be handled best by having some group sessions to talk over the newcomers to the neighborhood. If the practitioner succeeds in raising in the minds of the offenders some doubts about what they know about their new Negro neighbors, he may be able to get them to agree to have a few of the Negro boys come to a club meeting to tell about where they lived before and what it was like there. The practitioner now has a mixed group that he can perhaps organize more formally around some mutual interest, thus perpetuating the contacts that a friction incident created.

There seems to be little real knowledge about the merits of frank discussion in a mixed group of, for example, how it feels to be a Negro. While acknowledging that a "hush-hush" attitude toward the subject is bad, some practitioners feel that it should only be brought up "naturally," in the context of a specific incident. Others feel that inarticulate misconceptions and awkward feelings about racial or ethnic relationships merely perpetuate barriers to communication and feelings of social distance and discomfort. Undoubtedly, the answer in part depends on the age and maturity of the group that engages in such discussion. And if racial misconceptions are a real factor in a situation, surely there is something to be said for getting the real issue out on the table and working it through. But we know little of the best conditions for articulating and acknowledging prejudices, clarifying feelings, and airing suppressed tensions. Such conditions would undoubtedly involve some delicate balance between a genuinely permissive atmosphere and one in which the prevailing democratic norms of the American Creed—as represented in agency policy and the personal opinions of the practitioner—were explicit and known to all participants.

Since handling hostility and anger represents a normal area of professional concern for the group-work practitioner, the practitioner in intergroup relations should accept the hostility generated in racial and religious interaction without getting angry and losing his temper but by diagnosing the situation and treating it accordingly. His private feelings and prejudices need not interfere with the performance of his professional role. This applies especially to type B incidents (personal hostility present, intergroup antagonism absent).

Type B incidents undoubtedly require immediate handling to reaffirm the intergroup atmosphere. They probably also should involve some follow-up sessions in which the director can encourage a freer expression of the offenders' full feelings in the situation and decide what further steps, if any, need to be taken (e.g., a change of group, referral to a social agency, etc.).

Type D incidents (organized group scapegoating) are undoubtedly among the most difficult to handle. This kind of intergroup antagonism often reflects, or is reinforced by, peer-group associations and experiences outside the organization, such as gang fights or neighborhood conflicts. Although the authors feel that a limited part of the whole environment, such as a recreational center, can set its own policies, practices, and norms of conduct, this is difficult in the face of organized opposition. It undoubtedly requires fairly firm disciplinary controls within the organization and an alertness to the initial signs of trouble, and probably benefits considerably by good lines of communication among both adults and youth in the surrounding neighborhood.

In summary, let us repeat what we said at the beginning of this chapter: that desegregation is merely the process by which intergroup practices are changed in an institution or organization. It is not a goal in itself. The goal, also a process, is integration, for which changing the practices can only create the conditions. The extent to which an organization is achieving intergroup integration can best be measured by the effectiveness with which its practitioners use the nonsegregated environment to establish or reaffirm fair-play values in the participants.

PART II

Working for Better Intergroup Relations
in the Community at Large

CHAPTER 7

Realistic Goals for Community Action

A practitioner who would like to see general improvement in intergroup relations may want to extend his efforts beyond the particular institution or organization with which he is working, to work with others in the community to break down the barriers to full participation of minorities in all areas of community life. But with *whom* and *how* he works in the community depend on his philosophy of change in intergroup relations. In a community of considerable size, people are working through many different agencies and with many different techniques to improve intergroup relations. If practitioners are to use their time and effort most effectively in the community at large, they must decide what objectives they are going to move toward, with whom they will work, and what techniques they will use.

It is our belief that certain goals in intergroup relations are most realistic and that certain strategies and tactics most effectively accomplish these goals. Perhaps the biggest goal decision is deciding where to put the main emphasis: on attacking prejudice or on attacking discrimination. As a guide to a discussion of the various alternatives, a classification of the major types of intergroup action objectives and techniques might be helpful. Table 9 gives a schematic representation.

Attacking Prejudice

Many people feel that prejudice causes the basic ills of intergroup relations. They would argue that, until the basic attitudes of prejudiced people are changed, there can be no assurance of stable progress in intergroup relations and that

TABLE 9

THE MAJOR TYPES OF ACTION EFFORT IN INTERGROUP RELATIONS

Major Objective	Major Method	Techniques	Examples
These do not attack prejudice or discrimination		Wait for change	Set a good personal example in social circles and work relations Leave it up to time Get minority leaders to urge minority group to better itself
These attack prejudice	Exhortation and persuasion	Mass media	Use dramatic posters and exhibits in public places Use radio, television, and newspapers
		Personal exhortation	Arrange lectures, forums, etc., to interpret background and accomplishments of minority groups Urge clergymen to deliver sermons stressing tolerance
		Group process	Arrange discussion groups among parents to modify their attitudes Arrange educational courses for the public on intergroup relations

TABLE 9—Continued

Major Objective	Major Method	Techniques	Examples
These attack discrimination and segregation directly	Influencing strategic people by interpersonal relations	Motivate key people to attack discrimination	Arrange meetings between experts on intergroup relations and civic leaders Set up citizens' committees to study local situations and make recommendations
		Approach gatekeepers directly without invoking the law	Organize workshops for groups that handle intergroup situations in their work Let influential persons negotiate privately with discriminating establishments
	Influencing strategic people by applying sanctions	Bring in the law	Negotiate with legal violators to initiate better practices or face legal consequences Bring legal action against those who continue to practice discrimination
		Public pressure	Protest discrimination by open letters, petitions, and other publicity Organize boycotts or picketing of firms that discriminate

getting an individual employer here or a restaurant manager there to admit Negroes is just dealing with isolated symptoms of the problem. For they feel that prejudice is the basic problem and modifying prejudice the basic objective. As we have indicated, we believe that the more serious inequities suffered by minority groups can be alleviated best by directly attacking segregation and discrimination. But prejudice does interfere with good interpersonal relations. The more thoroughly misconceptions about minorities can be dispelled, the more feasible direct attacks on segregation and discrimination become.

But what can be done realistically to attack prejudices?[1] Every year hundreds of thousands of dollars are spent in head-on assaults on prejudice, by means of personal exhortation and persuasion or by the use of the mass media of communication. Yet we hardly know what targets this enormous barrage hits or what effect it has on the targets it does hit. One thing seems clear: those persons who are least prejudiced and who need it least are most likely to be exposed to exhortation. The prejudices that need modification are those of the "reluctant gatekeepers" who control the hiring practices of public and private employers, who stand in the way of Negro families trying to acquire decent homes, who make it difficult for minorities to obtain equal educational opportunities. But it is the rare reluctant gatekeeper who changes his practices because of a radio program, a magazine article, or a Brotherhood Week sermon—if, indeed, they even reach him. The principle suggested here is this:

PROPOSITION 19: *Attempts to modify prejudices by media that cannot counter the social pressures that perpetuate prejudice are not likely to be effective.*

1. The discussion that follows on attacking prejudice is intended to apply mainly to the general adult population on the community level. We do not refer to the educational processes of schools and other institutions dealing with young people in the formative years, where education for unprejudiced attitudes can be undeniably effective.

Of the three major methods of attacking prejudice, propaganda through the mass media is, of course, most likely to reach a broad public; but the stimulus to modify prejudices provided by most such propaganda is slight compared with more direct and personal means of persuasion and exhortation, such as lectures, sermons, and education through group processes. All three methods, however, undoubtedly serve to support the morale of minority persons and may provide some reinforcement to persons already working for better intergroup relations. They may have some slight effect in establishing a general atmosphere in which discrimination and prejudice against minorities is considered unfashionable, although there is little evidence to show that propaganda plays a major part in doing so.

To sum up, it is our feeling that it is difficult to make headway in improving intergroup relations by using personal exhortation and persuasion or the mass media of communication as principal tools. These methods can, however, reinforce, or give interpretation to, attitudes and ways of behaving learned through experience in a nonsegregated environment. As such, exhortation is a valuable, though limited, aid.

Attacking Segregation and Discrimination Directly

Direct attacks on segregation and discrimination often succeed because group traditions of fair play provide the basis for change. Most parts of the country now have an established and growing tradition of civil rights that applies without regard to race, creed, or national origin. We also have in this country a not-so-well-established but growing belief in "fair practices" in employment, housing, and social welfare. There appears to be an increasing acceptance of equality and fair play as a goal. Needless to say, there are wide differences of opinion as to how that goal can best be achieved. But one thing is clear: individuals and groups striving to perpetuate discrimination and segregation find it difficult morally to justify their position when it becomes defined as "unfair" or "unequal" or "denying the rights of . . . ."

When fair play or equal rights are well established in public policy, most people will go along with an enforcement of these policies by the proper authorities. Consequently, one of the most important strategies in intergroup relations is to get the intergroup goals of equality, fair play, and equal rights incorporated in public policy through legal ordinance or state regulations or by clearly enunciated public declarations of policy. The strategy is then to pry away at the practices that violate public policy by working through the duly constituted authorities.

An important part of the strategy is to avoid direct argument with violators as to what individual rights should be. Such definitions of rights and fair play are as numerous as social reformers—and as debatable, too. One cannot avoid arguing with judges and legislators and policy-makers about these rights. But persons in the public eye are reluctant to take a stand in declaring views in opposition to existing opinion; they will frequently go along with the enunciation and enactment of fair-play policies to avoid being on record against them.

PROPOSITION 20: *Successful efforts to eliminate segregation or discrimination usually have two phases: (1) getting fair-play policies established and (2) working to bring about compliance with and enforcement of these policies.*

For a policy to be firmly established, it needs (*a*) to be explicitly stated and (*b*) to be known to people on all levels who are strategic to its enforcement. In addition to these two requirements, a policy is more firmly established if (*c*) it is made known by public declaration.

Success in establishing fair-play *practices* on the local level depends heavily on two things: (1) The kind of local support that can be rallied behind fair-play *policies*. When there is strong state legislation and widespread community support of fair-play practices, there is the best chance of success. Whether there is state legislation or not, it will be necessary to organize substantial local support if fair-play policies are to be firmly established at the local level. Passive or tacit support by individuals here and there is not sufficient. (What constitutes effective community organization in intergroup relations action is discussed in the next chapter.) (2) How effective the sanctions are that can be brought to bear on reluctant gatekeepers to bring them into line with fair-play practices.

Because of the enormous variations in intergroup thinking from one state or region to another, decisions as to what constitute intergroup objectives for a particular community also vary widely. Fair-play objectives in areas of basic material welfare like jobs, housing, and educational opportunities are understandable and communicable to people in most American communities. But desegregating the swimming pools, for instance, may be a realistic objective in one community and wholly unrealistic in another. We include here brief sketches of three communities as they appeared to the Cornell research group in 1951, to give readers some feeling for the range of economic, political, and social organization within which intergroup action and goal decisions must be made.

COMMUNITY A: ÉLITEVILLE

Éliteville, in 1951, was an upper-class suburb of a large eastern city. It had no industry, almost no working-class population, and a large commuter element. Municipal administration and social service work were hobbies of the leisure class. Wealthy families contributed their professional and executive talents as "city fathers"; the social elite willingly put in time and effort for "good causes"; everyone was gracious and helpful. Much of the segregation that Éliteville revealed seemed to flow from a sort of social class snobbishness in which Italians, Jews, and Negroes "just aren't our type of people."

The old families, remembering when Éliteville was one of the wealthiest communities in the country, wanted to keep it a "nice" town, free from the infiltration of "inferior elements." The estates along upper Maple Avenue were exclusive enough by reason of their economic base, but just in case *nouveaux riches* Jews might try to move in, gentlemen's agreements held the line. One newly arrived Jewish attorney bought in by subterfuge, creating quite a fuss. A Jewish merchant, who regularly scanned the letterheads of the boards of directors of social agencies for a Jewish name, could not recall having run across one. This was one town where the Jewish community was *not* as well-to-do as the community at large; Jews were not invited on boards in exchange for large contributions. Middle-class Jews, Italians, and Negroes seemed peripheral to the life of the community.

The city commissioners, elected at large, were upper-class, public spirited citizens who took pride in their town and contributed their high talents for a pittance. No Jew or Negro had ever been a commissioner. City appointments were made only with the approval of a "Citizens' Committee on Appointments" dominated by "some of the very prominent people here."

In the social service field, too, the influence of the socially prominent families was apparent. Until about 1950, the Council of Social Agencies was run by a woman who paid exceeding deference to the elite and their social attitudes. The YWCA (with an all-colored clientele) and the neighborhood center (white staff, Italian-Negro clientele) were run *by* the ladies on the hill *for* the less fortunate families in the Fourth Ward. After an uphill fight of several years, during which the executive directorship of the Council of Social Agencies changed, the "uptown" people yielded some of their control over the budget and program of the Neighborhood Center to a Neighborhood Council with representation from the groups served.

Éliteville, whose Negro population was unusually large (20 per cent), illustrates how residential patterns underlie other patterns of segregation. It was said that the Negro community originally had supplied domestic labor for Éliteville's wealthy. Éliteville's reputation during the depression as a liberal relief and welfare town was said to have attracted more Negro families. The expanding Negro section occasionally opened new areas of settlement for Negroes, and the middle-class homes that became available were attractive to middle-class Negroes. Both white and Negro real estate operators took advantage of the status-striving motives of suburban families to capitalize, for their own profit, on the whites' fears of Negro invasion and property loss and the Negroes' aspirations for decent homes. School patterns, play patterns, and neighborhood patterns all reflected this segregation. Gentlemen's agreements reinforced it. The southwestern section of town was scarcely considered part of Éliteville by the upper classes. Christmas street decorations on the main street stopped short as Parker Avenue ran into the Negro section. Éliteville, to most commuting residents, meant "upper Éliteville" and "the hill."

COMMUNITY B: FACTORYTOWN

Factorytown, in 1951, was a heavily industrialized community of 65,000 lying between a large northern metropolis and a city bordering the South. The metropolis had segregated schools and many southern patterns; the border city had a local FEPC and many northern patterns. Factorytown's patterns were in the shadowy middle ground where it is often hard to tell what they are. Segregated schools had been ruled out, yet most of the schools were predominantly of one race. Both the YMCA and the YWCA ostensibly served all groups in the community, yet there were many signs of segregation. The American Federation of Teachers was one of the best-integrated organizations in town, yet Negro teachers taught only in all-Negro schools. Some plants had upgraded Negroes to the highest production jobs; others still refused to hire Negroes.

There was little leadership in the community working to weld these diverse practices into a liberal intergroup pattern with a philosophy of fair play to back it. The state had no fair employment practices law. Employers could still hire and fire as they pleased. The CIO had bucked the color line in many plants and in some had achieved real integration. During the war, when Factorytown was a frantic boom town, the federal FEPC, along with the unions, made rapid strides. But progress stalled when the plants cut back, and Negroes, because they were the last hired, were laid off in large numbers.

As an industrial town with street after street of old working-class homes, Factorytown offered few attractions to professional and managerial persons who earned their living there. Surrounding suburban areas had drained off persons who would have made responsible community leaders of vision and foresight. As one respondent said: "The motive in Factorytown is profit; no one wants to live there." The CIO had shown remarkable interest in certain community services and had organized an effective union counselor's training program; a few other agencies were making valiant efforts. But the centralization of community services in the county seat six miles away discouraged participation and contributed to a notable absence of community spirit.

As a result, major community responsibilities had long since fallen into the hands of a boss-controlled political machine, complete with patronage, graft, underworld protection, vote-buying, and a system of economic reprisals against the "unco-operative." So obvious was "the organization's" power to the citizens of Factorytown that 90 per cent of them registered the "boss's" party in 1950, although nearly a third actually *voted* the other party. The "organization" always won the major city and county posts, Factorytown residents voting heavily for the other party only in national presidential elections.

Although 20 per cent of the population was Negro, there were no Negro councilmen. The NAACP president ran once during the war on the Democratic ticket and lost. "He's one of the few who'll never sell us out," said one respondent. From all sides one heard that many leaders of the Negro community were "sell-outs." As one person put it: "The Negro leaders are bought and paid for by the Republican bosses." One way a Negro could make a decent living in Factorytown was to get into politics with the "organization." With "organization" protection, gambling joints, bootleg liquor, and houses of prostitution paid well. A few of the younger Negro men had tried to form a progressive league of independents, but they never successfully bucked the old-guard "organization" men, who were well intrenched. The result had been an apathetic "what's-the-use" attitude among the younger men which was not conducive to developing responsible leadership.

Although industrially advanced, Factorytown seemed to be at least a generation behind in community organization and leadership. Efforts to change intergroup patterns were sporadic and uneven; their success depended on the skills and persistence of individuals. The NAACP lacked needed Negro support and depended entirely on its long-time president and his personal effectiveness. The CIO had been effective in the plants it organized, but the intergroup policies of both CIO and AF of L had not been felt in other areas of community life. Factorytown languished in an apathy engendered in industrial blight, political corruption, and the default of responsible leaders.

COMMUNITY C: COMPANYTOWN

In 1951, Companytown Steel *was* Companytown. This border-south town's 25,000 inhabitants derived their economic sustenance from the mill. They were obligated to the mill, at least indirectly, for the roofs over their heads. Community recreational and medical facilities owed their very existence to the mill. Churches, lodges, schools, ball clubs—all were periodically enriched by substantial contributions from the mill. With its tax structure, the town could not possibly have balanced its budget and provided the services it did without the mill; and it was not surprising that Companytown citizens seemed to say, "All that I am and ever hope to be I owe to Samuel J. Murgatroyd" (president of Steel).

Companytown was a classic example of security by sufferance. The security of Companytown citizens did not accrue from a clearly established, impersonal system of rights and responsibilities, self-obtained, but existed because Companytown Steel had elected to play "Lord Bountiful," providing for the material, social, and cultural needs of its charges. So successful had this program been that Samuel J. Murgatroyd had twice been made mayor of the town by five-to-one majorities in free, nonpartisan elections. The CIO had failed repeatedly to win over the mill's "independent" union in honest, NLRB-supervised voting. In the Negro community, there was no effective NAACP. "Mr. Murgatroyd wouldn't like it."

In 1950, a patriotic foundation bestowed its highest award on Companytown for adherence to the American tradition of freedom. In a sense, this is not so surprising as it may seem. Companytown represented a triumph of benevolent despotism—the people liked it. It was not a police state in miniature; there was no outright coercion in Companytown. Workers in the mill were perfectly free to vote for the CIO. The CIO was, in fact, quite unable to substantiate charges against the company of intimidation in the previous year's labor-board election. The mill workers simply preferred the company union, and besides, "Mr. Murgatroyd doesn't like the CIO." Companytown citizens were not compelled to elect Murgatroyd mayor; he had opposition both times he ran. There was no law against an NAACP—simply no desire to activate one and no militant leaders to guide it.

Companytown's treasured freedom award was most seriously belied by the state of its Negro-white relations. These were mainly characterized by (1) almost total lack of integration of Negroes into the general life of the community and (2) lethargy and a fear-tinged complacency on the part of most Companytown Negroes. Much of this situation could be attributed to Companytown's southern locale and the southern origin of the bulk of its Negro population. But just as much it seemed to be a direct reflection of the company-dominated structure of the community. Companytown Negroes displayed the same Companytown Steel syndrome as Companytown's white citizens: they looked upon Samuel J. Murgatroyd as the giver of all good things; they were grateful for the material comforts and token representation in community affairs he bestowed; they regarded Companytown as the best of all possible places, since they, too, were isolated from the mainspring of modern society; they had developed no militant leadership, little conception of independent social action; they were stable, long-time residents, who owned their homes, and they didn't want to rock the boat.

Companytown Steel executives were fond of saying: "Our community is a good example of how the people of thirty-five nationalities, and the white man and the black, can work together in peace and harmony for over forty years without one single instance of racial trouble or discord." Companytown Steel executives acknowledged, however, that Negroes were not accorded equality of opportunity in the mill. "They aren't capable of doing the better jobs—they aren't educated," said the company's vice-president in charge of industrial relations. This might be related to the fact that, although the Negro youths almost inevitably ended up in the mill, there was absolutely no school training for a future life in Companytown—just a college-training curriculum. However, it was by no means rare for new white workers to be trained by these "uneducated" Negroes, then upgraded over the Negroes' heads. Colored workers were not upgraded except in certain least-favored, lowest-paying departments, where a few could be promoted to the top jobs. Most Negroes were hired on low-status jobs and remained there, regardless of seniority. They earned a good wage, but none were given the opportunity to qualify for the mill's top jobs.

Most employed Negroes had contributed to a new community center through payroll deductions, but the city still had not formulated a policy that told the Negroes they could use it. They were willing to settle for an "all-Negro night," but they did not know, as the center neared completion, that they would be permitted even that.

Realistic goals for intergroup action would obviously vary considerably among these communities. In choosing these objectives, a number of community variables must be borne in mind:

a) What are the basic community patterns of intergroup relations? Are they "southern," with many segregated facilities? Are they ambiguous, with no clear patterning? Are they largely northern, with most public facilities nonsegregated?

b) What is the basic socioeconomic structure and its relation to intergroup practices?

c) What are the possibilities for involving influential leaders in support of a given intergroup relations objective?

d) What is the nature of the minority leadership?

e) What is the general effectiveness of ongoing intergroup relations action organizations in the community?

f) Who are the key gatekeepers in various sectors of community life, and what is their intergroup relations position?

g) What are the available negative sanctions that can be brought to bear, especially legal sanctions embodied in state or local civil-rights or fair employment practices legislation?

Before moving along to a discussion of the strategy of community organization and action efforts in intergroup relations, let us compare briefly the three communities we have just described in each of these variables (see Table 10).

Dissecting the communities as shown in Table 10 makes possible at least a tentative selection of realistic intergroup goals for each setting. In Éliteville, where majority-group community leaders are public spirited and responsible, an immediate objective might be to work with some of these leaders as well as with the few interested minority leaders, to broaden minority participation in the community's social agency structure. This might, in turn, lead to the involvement of these community leaders in longer-range intergroup objectives, such as improved housing for Negroes on a less segregated basis. In Factorytown, a realistic objective would be further integration of Negroes into the major plants. NAACP leaders and CIO officials might form the nucleus of an action organization, with the possibility of support for the objective from the local newspaper. Negro members of the political organization would hesitate to oppose such an objective, and both Negro and white politicians might see political advantage in it. While Companytown presents the least optimistic picture, company officials do take pride in what they see as the embodiment in Companytown of the American "melting-pot" tradition. A realistic goal might be to reactivate Negro leaders around the issue of wider Negro participation in the community's recreational facilities, with special reference to the new community center. The main leverage would be the fact of Negro financial support and company officials' stated adherence to the "melting-pot" principle.

In each community setting a different strategy may be best

TABLE 10

	Eliteville	Factorytown	Companytown
Community intergroup pattern	Northern: little segregation	Mixed: some northern, some southern patterns	Basically southern, with much segregation
Socioeconomic structure and leadership	Fashionable suburban, with responsible leadership	Diversified industrial, with hardheaded economic and political leadership	One-company town, with company leaders heading major community projects
Potential involvement of key leaders	Good	Only for practical political and economic advantage	Poor—too conservative
Minority leadership	Middle-class; poorly organized; a few effective individuals	Mostly subservient to political and economic power; a few effective individuals	Subservient to company leadership
Effectiveness of action organizations	Largely inactive, with sporadic signs of life	Effective NAACP and CIO leadership, with weak support; sporadic efforts elsewhere	Nil
Key gatekeepers	Real estate operators, commercial leaders, social agency leaders	Political leaders, plant managers, school authorities	Company officials
Available negative sanctions	Good legal sanctions in employment, education, and public accommodations; little else	Good legal sanctions in public accommodations; friendly newspaper; effective labor organizations	Extra-community publicity; otherwise only moral sanctions

in selecting and organizing to achieve realistic intergroup objectives; the strategy should be tailor-made to suit local peculiarities in community structure and function. Only persons who are intimately concerned with the inner workings of a community's life are in a position to choose realistic objectives and design strategy. Any individuals or groups planning action on a community-wide basis should consult such strategic individuals. Efforts to achieve unrealistic goals, undertaken without the participation of leaders insightful in community processes, are almost certainly doomed to failure.

Since the selection of goals clearly involves the consideration of organization to achieve these goals, our next question becomes: What is the pattern of effective community organization for action in intergroup relations?

CHAPTER 8

The Pattern of Effective Community Organization

In most American communities we can delineate a number of different subcultures or organizational networks that have their own leadership structure, institutions, lines of communication and authority, and perhaps even their own customs and mores. There is the network of social agencies, the legal and judicial structure, the educational system, the Jewish community, the Negro community, the health and medical complex, the business and chamber of commerce group, the real estate and mortgage interests, and so on. Each of these segments of community life functions as a sort of subsystem, interacting and overlapping with other segments. But many of them are drawn together at the top by interlocking leaderships that represent what we might call the "power structure" of the community. In a community of fifty to a hundred thousand people an "inner core" of perhaps a dozen individuals plus a peripheral group of perhaps fifty to one hundred more will make most of the decisions on significant community affairs. Even if they do not make the decisions themselves, others will be inclined to "clear" with them before taking action or, at least, be fearful of taking action which they think might offend the key leaders.

This situation poses a dilemma for persons interested in action in intergroup relations. Should they work with the people who are already strongly motivated in support of better intergroup relations but who, perhaps, are not influential in the community? Or should they try to motivate and involve key community leaders who might go along with a better intergroup relations program but who, perhaps, at present are unaware of, or not interested in, intergroup relations?

It appears that in most communities, the people really dedicated to better intergroup relations are not influential leaders in the community. Persons most likely to have been bitten by the intergroup relations "bug" seem to be schoolteachers, clergymen, social workers, minority leaders, and an occasional private citizen of good will. Respected though these people are, in our society they rarely wield an influence comparable to that of leaders in industry, business, or "society."

But in many communities there are persons in the power structure who are sympathetic to fair-play policies. In many sections of the country intergroup relations has become a good "cause" for conservatives to be liberal about. It is not basically threatening to their own economic or social status in the community and meets all the requirements of moral rectitude. Being "for" good intergroup relations is like being against sin. In southern communities, also, there are citizens of influence who will support certain limited intergroup objectives. The main controversies, whatever the region, revolve around how much, how fast, and how far we should proceed.

Where in the community structure can we find persons of influence who might become motivated in support of improved intergroup relations? Naturally, this varies from one community to another, but frequently a good place to start looking is among the up-and-coming younger leaders who are not yet overburdened with community responsibility and who might respond to opportunities for leadership in a good cause. It is often helpful to consult older, better-established community leaders about younger business or professional men who might be most interested and able. Suggestions coming from an "elder statesman" in the local community may be just the encouragement a young leader needs to agree to participate in an intergroup action program.

Naturally, anyone approached to participate in support of

a cause about which he knows little will hesitate to be drawn in; direct requests of this sort are likely to be refused. An approach that is sometimes successful is for a small delegation to solicit the advice of an influential leader about strategy in an area of community life with which he is familiar. Most people are gratified to be asked their advice on community affairs and will give it willingly. It follows that, in order to give good advice about strategy, the leader must assume the point of view and objectives of the delegation, thus starting the process of identification and involvement. To give good advice, the leader must also ask certain questions about the intergroup relations problems involved, and this begins his education and enlightenment on the seriousness of these problems in the local community.

Giving advice may help the leader to become ego-involved. A person who gives advice tends to develop a stake in seeing that his advice works. He may be motivated to pull a few strings personally. It will be easy to keep him in touch with how things are proceeding or perhaps have him attend a meeting to discuss the situation further. After a few meetings that have exposed him to close contact with and greater knowledge of the intergroup situation, he may even become identified with the problem and anxious for its solution. Actually, we know little about the process by which such persons become emotionally involved in intergroup relations objectives. But in our research we have found that it takes place in community after community, and we have observed that where it does occur, movement toward the intergroup objective is more rapid and decisive than where it does not.

In pointing out the importance of motivating influential leaders, we do not imply that the originally motivated people below the top leadership level in the community are not equally vital to the achievement of intergroup relations objectives. These people form the hard core of intergroup action in any community. Without them, no movement could occur, and the question of motivating others would be academic: this dedicated nucleus does the motivating. Our point is simply this, given an initially motivated group:

PROPOSITION 21: *Community-wide action in intergroup relations is more often successful when strategic, influential community leaders participate at the outset in the planning and organization of the action effort.*

Let us assume now that the action group has managed to motivate a few really influential people in the community and that a small executive committee has been organized on which they are represented. What are the next steps in community action?

The small working committee should probably look toward the formation of some more widely representative community committees that will work for the establishment of fair-play policies on the community level. Three types of committee suggest themselves as possibilities: (1) an *ad hoc* legislative committee to work for the incorporation of fair-play policies in city or state ordinances; (2) a city-wide policy committee, such as a mayor's commission or a council for civic unity; and (3) an exploratory committee to investigate the current status of intergroup relations and make subsequent recommendations. Which of these committees will be most appropriate depends on the status of intergroup relations in the community, local leaders' knowledge about the situation, and the nature of existing statutes and ordinances. At different stages of time or strategy, one type may be more appropriate than another. The most logical progression would be from an exploratory committee to a policy committee to the formation of an *ad hoc* legislative committee. Let us look briefly at the functions of these three.

The Exploratory Committee

Exploratory committees vary all the way from a working committee of key people to a full-blown community self-survey or self-audit. The working principle that underlies exploratory committees is this:

PROPOSITION 22: *Exploration of a local intergroup relations problem often supplies key people with convincing evidence of the seriousness of the problem and brings home the need for action.*

In the self-survey or self-audit, the influential people that one hopes will lead the action efforts participate actively in the gathering of data.[1] They are in a position to form policy and establish action objectives on the basis of the information that they have gathered themselves. This guarantees that the objectives laid down for action will be in line not only with local circumstances but also with the sophistication, level of militancy, and pace of local leadership. It is an obvious but important fact that community-wide action can go no more rapidly than local leaders are willing to move.

Perhaps the main danger of exploratory committees is that they sometimes threaten key people in the areas of community life they investigate. Suppose, for instance, that a small exploratory committee were to examine the real estate practices involving intergroup relations in a community. If there was a tacit agreement among real estate men not to rent or sell homes to Negro families in predominantly white neighborhoods, any investigation that threatened to bring this information to light would draw the united opposition of the real estate men. The self-survey hopes to avoid this problem by involving the key real estate people in the fact-finding stages of the inquiry. As a result of the exploratory work, the key participating individuals in each area of community life, in this case the real estate men, may become motivated to take a greater amount of re-

1. See Claire Selltiz and Margot Haas Wormser (eds.), "Community Self-surveys: An Approach to Social Change," *Journal of Social Issues,* spring, 1949; see also M. H. Wormser and C. Selltiz, *How To Conduct a Community Self-survey of Civil Rights* (New York: Association Press, 1951.

sponsibility for the intergroup injustices occurring in the area of community life with which they are most deeply concerned. It is on this sense of deepened responsibility that the action group must rely for its leverage in future community action.

Any report that an exploratory committee might produce that recommended direct and immediate changes in many areas of community life would probably be strongly resisted. Perhaps the best outcome of an exploratory committee's work would be (a) a wider awareness of the seriousness of the problem on the part of key leaders and (b) a recommendation for the establishment of a more permanent committee to go to work on these problems. An exploratory committee might recommend the formation of a mayor's commission or a council for civic unity (i.e., a city-wide policy committee).

A City-wide Policy Committee

A city-wide policy committee has three major functions:

a) Promoting City Legislation

In communities located in states with little or no civil-rights or fair employment practices legislation, city ordinances are the best way to establish fair-play policies. A policy committee working toward certain legislative goals will probably find it advantageous to stay largely in the background. Its major function might be to help organize a temporary *ad hoc* citizens' committee formed for this specific legislative objective (see below).

b) Establishing Fair-Play Policy in Various Segments of Community Life

In states or cities having fair employment practices or civil-rights laws, a mayor's commission or a council for civic unity should not be a fire department that puts out every conflagration set off by intergroup relations tensions. Individual grievances should be handled through appropriate procedures. If a person has a complaint about discrimination in employment, the state fair employment practices commission is the appropriate group to handle it. If an individual has been discriminated against in some public place, such as a refusal of service in a restaurant, the NAACP can legitimately bring the violator of the civil-rights statute to court. The function of a policy committee in these circumstances is to see that the local firms and places of public accommodation have clearly established policies that are nondiscriminatory. Where there is no recourse to law, a city-wide policy committee may find it necessary to set up subcommittees that would investigate grievances; their findings could serve as a basis for working toward corrective municipal ordinances.

You may ask: If there is unequivocal state legislation covering civil-rights and fair employment policy, isn't community policy already established by state law? Not necessarily, if by "established policy" we bear in mind the three criteria cited in an earlier chapter: an explicit statement of the policy, well-informed people on all levels who are strategic to the policy's enforcement, and a public declaration of the policy. We have observed a number of communities where there was discrimination both in employment and in upgrading of Negroes in industrial firms despite the existence of unequivocal state legislation and, in some cases, a mayor's commission as well.

How would a mayor's commission go about establishing fair-play policies in employment on a local level? There are various approaches, but the following might be as feasible as any. If the personnel of the mayor's commission has been carefully selected, it should have several members strategic to employment and personnel work. For instance, the mayor's commission of one eastern community has on its board the managers of two large plants and executives from several others. Suppose at the board's request the mayor were to appoint three of these persons to an exploratory subcommittee to investigate how fair employment practices could be more firmly established in the community.

These three members might, after conferring with one another, then invite three or four more persons not on the mayor's commission to join with them. These persons should be the individuals they deem most strategic to employment and personnel work in the community. This exploratory committee of six or seven people would then meet over a period of weeks to determine what course of action might be most fruitful in accomplishing their objectives. Perhaps they would decide that a series of larger meetings (institutes or workshops) be set up for persons engaged in personnel work.

If a workshop is decided on, then all the techniques of running a successful workshop would come into play. For example: committees could be appointed to plan and run the various sections of the workshop or institute meetings; these committees would be selected in such a way as to involve as many additional strategic personnel men as possible. The main learning processes in a workshop actually take place in the committee, where the planning is done. The workshop itself would serve primarily as the high point for reinforcement of the participants' values in the field of fair employment practices. Hopefully, at the final meeting of the workshop, a resolution would be passed making a public declaration of the intention of the workshop participants (including all the major firms of the area) to promote fair employment practices.

Certain procedures for establishing fair-play practices at all levels of employment would have come out of the working sessions of the workshop. For example, certain personnel men might have decided to prepare for their manager's signature a directive to be sent to all department heads, unit heads, supervisors, and foremen, declaring the firm intention of the organization to maintain fair employment practices. If all these things have been done, we can then agree that fair-play *policies* have been established in this area of community life.

Similar procedures would be in order for other areas of community life, such as restaurants and taverns, hotel administration, department-store personnel, theater management, classroom practice, and vocational counseling in the schools and any other aspects of community life where fair-play policy needs to be more firmly established.

c) Establishing a Favorable Community-wide Atmosphere

In addition to specific area projects directly attacking discrimination and segregation, a city-wide policy committee can do much to establish an over-all community atmosphere in which social change toward better intergroup relations can thrive. As we pointed out before, just how much headway can be made in promoting a better climate of opinion in intergroup relations is questionable. But by a strategic use of mass media and public functions, the committee can constantly reinforce the democratic values of people interested in doing something about intergroup relations and may possibly inhibit the antidemocratic tendencies of reluctant gatekeepers. Making intergroup relations awards that acknowledge the major steps in community progress can draw favorable newspaper publicity and involve various strategic people. Outstanding achievements of minority leaders can be publicized. Brotherhood Week or other intergroup celebrations can be made occasions for bringing to the community's attention notable intergroup relations achievements. Although things like this may not get a single Negro a job or break down a single discrimination barrier, they do change the atmosphere always more firmly in favor of the traditions of civil rights and fair play that give local action groups their main leverage in the community.

The Legislative Committee

There are various types of legislative committees, but one of the most useful in working for a given piece of legislation is what we might call the "temporary *ad hoc* citizens' committee," for example, a city-wide citizens' committee for fair employment practices. Busy persons of high standing in the community will often lend their names and support to a temporary committee but not to a permanent one which might make them feel saddled with a continuing obligation that they could not discharge. The citizens' committee can be larger than would be manageable for a working committee that had to get things done over a long period of time. The personnel of the citizens' committee can be planned so as to give representation to all the groups in the community that can be brought to support the objective.

Naturally, the working core of a large citizens' committee will have to be a handful of loyal and dedicated persons. They should probably work behind the scenes. A major objective of the working core should be to rally as much organizational support for the legislation as possible. Organizational support has a special characteristic: it gives the impression of rank-and-file, grass-roots, mass support, since most of us attribute to the action of an organization the indorsement of the membership in its full complement, even when only a handful of the leadership participates in the decision. Thus widespread organizational support can be highly effective in legislative campaigns. City-wide citizens' committees can also be the organizational focus of public meetings or rallies where key legislators are put on the record for intergroup relations causes; most public officials will hesitate to go on the record on the side of injustice and inequality.

Because of its loose organization and temporary status, the *ad hoc* committee has a flexibility and maneuverability much greater than organizations that are well institutionalized. All in all, the *ad hoc* committee is an important action technique for the intergroup relations practitioner to be aware of.

Working with Existing Action Organizations

In most communities of any size, the major action efforts to establish fair-play policies are made by organizations either directly or indirectly interested in intergroup relations. In many instances the individual practitioner is not in a position to establish new city-wide committees, perhaps for lack of time or because a new committee's objectives would overlap or even coincide with those of existing organizations. The problem, then, is: How can the practitioner work most effectively with existing action organizations?

He can do three things: (a) appraise the effectiveness of existing organizations, (b) establish the most feasible working relationships with such organizations, to expedite what he feels are the essential intergroup objectives, and (c) be instrumental in implementing new organizational forms or machinery for co-ordinating different action efforts in the community.

a) Evaluating Effectiveness of Existing Action Organizations

We have found it useful to evaluate certain aspects of action organizations to determine their effectiveness. These are: (1) organizational structure, (2) participation, (3) effectiveness of prime movers, and (4) major accomplishments or failures.

1. *Organizational structure.*—In an analysis of organizational structure, it is helpful to consider the following questions: Is the organization an official or an unofficial body? Is it autonomous or a local branch of a national organization? Is intergroup relations its primary concern or a peripheral interest? What is its source of funds?

Is the organization an official or an unofficial body? Official organizations may find politics intruding into the situation; certain limits may be put on their activities by the public officials or the mandate under which they operate. For example, if an official mayor's commission begins to go after the fire department for not hiring Negro firemen, the fire commissioner or chief might very well object. He might go to the mayor and say: "Look here, what's this mayor's commission of yours doing, trying to tell us how to run our business. If there's much more of this, I'll resign." Or the fire commissioner may apply pressure in other politically powerful areas and may actually jeopardize the mayor's position in terms of support and subsequent re-election. The mayor may find it expedient to call the director of the mayor's commission and say: "Perhaps we had better forget about the fire department now. We'll get around to that later. The fire commissioner is raising a row, and it might be wise to keep peace in the family."

In a private or unofficial organization, such a situation is less likely to occur. Although, by coincidence, the intergroup relations organization might step on the toes of someone who is close to a committee member, the unofficial organization is not structurally exposed to political pressures as is the official group. This, of course, does not mean that the practitioner interested in improving intergroup relations in his community should avoid official organizations. It means only that he needs an awareness of the kinds of limitations on intergroup action that a political or quasi-political body faces. On the other hand, the very official status of such an organization frequently gives it leverage and prestige that many unofficial or private organizations do not possess.

Is the group autonomous or a local branch of a national organization? National organizations that have clearly established intergroup relations policies provide a source of leverage that can be used to get movement in intergroup relations on the part of a local chapter. Some national organizations have intergroup relations experts, who prepare materials of use to the local staff, help organize local workshops, or confer with local leaders on their special community problems.

Many national organizations provide special intergroup training for the professionals who will staff their local chapters. Where such training is well planned and extensive, the local leader appears to evaluate his professional progress on the basis of national standards. To the extent that these become important reference points for the local staff member, we can expect him to give leadership to his board and other local community people in intergroup relations. If, on the other hand, the national organization does not establish itself and what it expects firmly in the mind of its local professionals but leaves them largely autonomous, then the local professionals will tend to set their patterns of intergroup relations in conformity with other local practices rather than ahead of them. This appears to be a major reason why two organizations with apparently parallel programs can differ considerably in their effectiveness in getting movement in intergroup relations.

C. Is intergroup relations the organization's primary concern or a peripheral interest? The rather obvious point to be made here is that the organization with only a peripheral interest in intergroup relations is less likely to be doing something about it than one with intergroup relations as its primary concern. In the former case, even if the executives are motivated enough to take action, they are less likely to be as sophisticated in intergroup relations strategy as the professionals for whose organization these are the main objectives.

d. What is the organization's source of funds? Organizations that get their funds from the Community Chest, for instance, may feel that they cannot use militant or forthright methods in working for their intergroup objectives. Militancy may make an organization controversial or may alienate certain key people in the community; consequently, the next request for funds may be turned down. Such vulnerability can be overcome in part by building community support based on participation.

2. *Participation.*—As indicated earlier, the effectiveness of an action organization depends heavily on who the participants are. In order to establish policy or bring about compliance in various segments of community life, an organization needs to involve in its program strategic people from each different area. Such representation provides leverage for intergroup relations action. In addition, a city-wide organization will probably want participation from at least a few highly influential leaders in the community, members of the legal profession, and representatives of the various minority groups.

It is important that a board of this sort represent a considerable range of opinion and sophistication in intergroup relations. But an overrepresentation of inexperienced and conservative participants may hold back the group from realizing intergroup objectives. A widely representative group is desirable in terms of realizing objectives.

PROPOSITION 23: *Social conflict on an intergroup relations issue, if successfully resolved, usually leads to further movement toward better intergroup relations.*

It is important to note the word "successfully"; the conflict situation has to be carefully guided to make sure that the resolution is successful. Through discussion and involvement, the conservative or naïve participants are likely to become aware of their naïveté, and, in order not to appear so, they will go along with the prevailing temper of the group. Since intergroup relations objectives are morally unassailable, going along with such movements is to be on the "side of the angels." Since the objectives are indisputable, differences are likely to revolve, instead, about strategies, and here the more sophisticated members can give leadership.

3. *Effectiveness of prime movers.*—Most action organizations are really run by a handful of motivated persons who have established a working relationship among themselves; sometimes a single individual or two supply the essential leadership of this hard "inner core." By discussing various projects of the organization with board members or other individuals, it is possible to discover rapidly who these persons are. Their effectiveness in giving leadership to the organization and in accomplishing its action objectives depends on a number of things.

An effective prime mover needs to have a substantial amount of time and effort to devote to the organization. This may seem perfectly obvious, but it must not be forgotten. Many of the most influential leaders in a community are working full time and are burdened with many other community responsibilities.

They just cannot give the time and effort required to accomplish significant intergroup relations objectives. The most effective prime movers we have come across in our community studies were people such as these: a young Negro army officer who had been pensioned because of a bad heart and who could devote virtually full time to the NAACP chapter, of which he was president; a free-lance writer in a southwestern city who could take off a week or so to lobby in the state legislature at a crucial time; a clubwoman whose children were past school age and who thus had plenty of time to devote to community affairs.

An effective prime mover needs to be strongly motivated in the cause of intergroup relations. Many individuals articulate a strong motivation, but when it comes to the test of working long hours at sometimes tedious duties, their motivation turns out to be paper-thin. Frequently, too, other motivations become involved in action efforts in intergroup relations: one may participate in exciting conferences and meetings; one may get into the limelight; as a minority leader, one may gain status in the minority group for being active; one may have wide opportunities to mix with persons of high standing in the majority community. If fighting hard for intergroup relations objectives threatens these other motivations, the real strength of intergroup motivation will come out. The Negro community has a term for an individual with genuine motivation: a "race man."

An effective prime mover needs to be an effective operator in interpersonal situations. Many intergroup relations leaders are "successful" in that they can participate congenially and do not antagonize people. By an "operator" we mean someone who not only is successful in this sense but also is "effective" in getting some movement out of the interpersonal situation. An effective "operator" is able to motivate people and win their confidence. He can mitigate irrelevant irritations that arise, can make constructive use of tension in a charged interpersonal situation, and can interpret delicate situations with a positive feeling tone. He makes appropriate use of the leverage he has in the situation, so that he does not antagonize and become disruptive but does make perfectly clear the implications of ignoring that leverage.

This may sound like an unrealistic set of criteria, but there are effective operators of this kind in most communities. Such an individual can usually be spotted fairly easily: he is the person that the other leaders want to "clear with" before taking steps in some matter; he is the person to whom people account for important actions they undertake; at the same time he has the knack of getting them to assume responsibility for taking action and to consult him only on major decisions.

An effective prime mover needs to be sophisticated in the strategy and tactics of intergroup relations. There are many leaders in intergroup relations who fill all the other requirements of an effective prime mover but who, because of their misunderstanding of what works to get movement and what does not, cannot be truly effective.

An effective prime mover needs to be free of sanctions that can be invoked to make him back down. Although no individual is completely free of sanctions, certain types are more powerful than others. We have in mind such crippling situations as clergymen may find themselves in, when they lead churches where the parish has considerable say about who their pastor will be. We have come across instances in which a clergyman interested in intergroup relations was threatened with the loss of his parish if he persisted in pursuing his "radical" intergroup objectives. Lawyers who may lose significant accounts if they vigorously pursue intergroup relations objectives are in danger of being "sanctioned" out of their effectiveness. Schoolteachers or other public officials on the lower levels may be seriously hampered by sanctions, for political pressure can be brought to bear on their administrative heads to back down on a crucial issue. In one instance some schoolteachers who were advisers to an interracial club saw no objection to interracial dancing or dating for an important school dance. But when the school superintendent brought sharp pressure to bear on these teachers to see that no such dancing occurred, they felt compelled to go along with him; their jobs were at stake.

Conversely, a retired person with an independent income or an individual who is his own boss is hard to obstruct by the use of sanctions of this kind. But even here the economic or social ties of his relatives may serve as points of leverage where negative sanctions can be applied. Social ostracism is sometimes employed as an effective sanction; needless to say, a leader who finds himself socially ostracized loses considerably in effectiveness.

It is appropriate here to say a few words about the role of the professional intergroup relations practitioner as the prime mover of an intergroup relations organization. We feel that the professional who becomes the overt leader of an intergroup organization threatens his own effectiveness.

The professional wants to maintain the full support of his policy board, which, in the best cases, is a mixture of conservatives and liberals, of militants and gradualists, of sophisticates and naïves. If the professional initiates the contacts in the community, undertakes the negotiations personally, invokes the sanctions necessary to get movement on particular issues, he is bound to antagonize numbers of people. Individual board members will undoubtedly be made aware of community sentiment and will find themselves in a difficult position: they may support the professional, or they may side with their friends in the community who object to what the professional is doing. If the decision is in favor of the board members' friends, the board will be split. A board split on the issue may be in danger of losing the more conservative and less militant members. Even if the board does not split, its members will be likely to scrutinize the professional's future actions with a somewhat jaundiced eye.

Suppose the professional operates in this way instead: When

a controversial issue arises, he brings it to the attention of the board and says that he thinks it deserves consideration. After preliminary discussion, a committee of three is appointed to explore the problem and make recommendations for action. The small committee, composed of a representative sample of the board, with the professional acting as a resource person, proceeds to examine the problem. The members of the small group will benefit from the experience of discussing the controversial issue and formulating their stand. After investigation and deliberation, the committee goes back to the board with a recommendation for action. If the committee decision is a consensus, the conservative board members are in no position to criticize the professional for his action. Since the small committee was originally set up with conservative as well as liberal members, the conservatives will play an important part in convincing other conservatives on the board of the soundness of the decision. The controversial issue thus tends to unify rather than divide the group; the board members are given an opportunity to arrive at the point of view by themselves. When the time comes to explain the position of the committee to friends and relatives, each board member feels that this is a "group" decision, and feels more secure in his stand.

4. *Major accomplishments or failures.*—We can learn a great deal about an organization by examining the projects it undertakes. We can see whether the prime movers of the organization pick realistic goals for their action projects. We can determine how successful the prime movers have been in involving influential persons in the strategic areas of action. We can also judge the appropriateness of specific strategy and tactics involved in the action project for a particular situation or community context. Projects that were failures are especially illuminating in each of these respects.

In the light of these criteria for evaluating the effectiveness of action organizations, let us take a look at three concrete instances of city-wide policy committees that had different degrees of success.

THE VALLEYTOWN MAYOR'S COMMITTEE
ON HUMAN RELATIONS

For several years, a number of organizations and individuals in the small northeastern city of Valleytown had staged an annual Brotherhood Week dinner. These functions were always well attended, but many participants felt that their influence on the total community, if any, was too superficial and transitory to be permanently valuable. They believed that Valleytown needed a permanent working committee with wide community representation that could survey the city's intergroup relations needs and work out a realistic action program. They knew that although Valleytown was located in a state that had clear civil-rights and fair employment practices legislation, many of the city's actual intergroup practices failed by a wide margin to measure up to public policy as the laws defined it.

One year, some time before Brotherhood Week, several members of the planning committee conceived the idea of requesting the mayor, through a resolution to be passed at the Brotherhood Week dinner, to form a mayor's committee that would deal exclusively with intergroup relations problems on the local community level. A resolution was drafted and passed unanimously at the Brotherhood Week dinner. The committee that drew up the resolution, already representative of three ethnic groups and four occupational groups (clergy, social work, university, small business), met with the mayor and found him interested and co-operative; The Valleytown Mayor's Committee on Human Relations was born.

Initially, the mayor's committee consisted of thirteen members selected by the mayor in consultation with the original Brotherhood Week planning committee. Religious, racial, and foreign-extraction groups were well represented, but important occupational groups and key community leadership were not. The business community was represented by two men, both of whom operated small firms employing a handful of people. Only three professions—social work, education, and law—were represented. There was no representation at all from the city's labor organizations. But within a few months, the committee decided to expand to include strategic people from local industry and retailing firms. The plant managers of two large factories joined the committtee, along with the owners of the city's two leading department stores. Ultimately, the committee doubled its original size, adding a union leader and a few more businessmen. But in the first few months of its operations, the mayor's committee was both inadequately representative of community leadership and relatively inactive.

This initial inactivity was not wasted time, however. In the early months, committee members were learning about each other, breaking through communication barriers that resulted from their varying racial and religious origins. White members were learning, for example, that minstrel shows were offensive to many Negroes. Gentiles were learning that many Jews experienced deep hurt over the social exclusion practiced by some organizations in the community. Negroes were learning that other minority groups had problems similar to theirs. The first few months spent "just talking" seemed to serve as a catharsis for the committee, transforming it into a real working group and unifying it for future action efforts.

And action did begin to occur. Toward the end of its first year, the mayor's committee set up a series of specific objectives based on a survey made earlier by a subcommittee of its members. These fell into four broad categories: (1) increasing economic opportunity for Negroes; (2) promoting fuller utilization of social service facilities by Negroes; (3) opening up public housing projects to Negroes; (4) opening up the city's service clubs to Negro members. The committee had made the broad decision that since the Negro minority was the most seriously deprived in Valleytown, it would concentrate its major efforts on widening opportunities for that group.

The mayor's committee subsequently made real progress in each of these areas. It worked with the local housing authority to get a Negro family admitted into a previously all-white project and to make sure that a newly constructed project was interracial from the beginning. It worked with the management of the local telephone company to get qualified Negro operators into the work force. It obtained membership for Negroes in at least one of Valleytown's service clubs and worked with a settlement house to get Negro representation on the board of directors. It gave moral support to a visiting nurses' group in its decision to employ a Negro on its professional staff. A committee of its members organized and conducted a workshop on intergroup relations for group and recreation workers from Valleytown and other cities in the state.

Probably the mayor's committee's most significant achievement was its successful negotiation with the local school authorities to get Negro teachers into the public school system for the first time in the city's history. All members of the mayor's committee were agreed that this was a legitimate and desirable objective, and one the community was certainly not organized against. The problem was to persuade the gatekeepers—in this case the board of education and superintendent of schools—that there *was* a problem and that it should be remedied as soon as possible. The approach was direct: the mayor invited the entire board of education and the superintendent of schools to meet with him and his Committee on Human Relations to discuss the feasibility of integrating Negro teachers into the public school system.

The meeting began with a general policy statement by the chairman of the board. He said that all applicants for teaching jobs were given equal consideration, regardless of race, creed, or color. There simply had been no Negro applicants, he said, for which the board could hardly be held responsible. But during the discussion that followed, it became apparent to everyone that in actual practice all applicants were *not* given equal consideration. For one thing, graduates of the local school system were often given preference over applicants from other cities, particularly if they knew the "right people." It developed, too, that a few Negroes actually had completed application papers but had never filed them because they had been led to believe by school officials or teachers that their applications would be refused, that the time was not yet "ripe" for hiring Negro teachers, or that the first Negro teacher should be someone with "outstanding" qualifications.

The discussion made clear to members of both the mayor's committee and the board of education that a subtle form of discrimination had been practiced and that if it continued, no Negroes at all were likely to be hired into the system in the foreseeable future. Board of education policy was clearly against discrimination, and no board member wanted to seem to defy that policy, particularly now that it was out in the open before a semiofficial civic body. At this point, someone pointed out that a Negro college student was currently doing his practice teaching in one of the local schools. He was, according to the superintendent, only "fair," in no way outstanding. He conceded, however, that white applicants with similar qualifications and background had been hired. Was the difference, asked a mayor's committee member, that this man was a Negro? The board of education realized that this seemed to be the implication. A few days later, the superintendent of schools talked with the Negro practice teacher and found he was interested in a permanent appointment in Valleytown. When the fall semester began, the city had its first Negro teacher, and has since added at least one more.

For a brief period, following its initial successes, the mayor's committee found itself functioning as a grievance committee, handling specific complaints of discrimination in public places brought by individuals in the community. Since the state had both fair employment and civil-rights laws and since Valleytown had a fairly active branch of the NAACP, some committee members felt the mayor's committee should refer such cases to the appropriate agencies and should concentrate its own efforts toward opening new areas of opportunity for Negroes and getting firm policy commitments from key gatekeepers in the community.

The Valleytown mayor's committee made least progress in the area of industrial employment and upgrading of Negroes. Valleytown is a highly industrial city, with both absentee- and locally owned plants. Although most of these plants hired Negroes, some were reluctant to upgrade them into supervisory positions, some tended to segregate them into low-paying, heavy-work departments, and a few employed them only as janitors and restroom matrons. Since Valleytown's Negro population was predominantly working class, this type of discrimination was a serious hardship. Although the state had a Fair Employment Practices Commission, Valleytown Negroes had usually "solved" their employment problems by resigning themselves to low-rated jobs or by commuting to other industrial centers where opportunities for promotion were better. A legitimate mayor's committee function would have been to organize a conference or workshop for local industrial and union leaders, to work out a hiring and employment policy that would be fair and as uniform as possible. Or the mayor's committee could have appointed a subcommittee to work continuously on this specific problem. But the committee never faced the industrial employment situation squarely, nor did it ever include among its members many gatekeepers from management and unions who were in a strong position to improve the situation.

A unique feature of this mayor's committee was that in its early stages it was closely associated with a university research group studying intergroup relations in Valleytown. Members of this research group were instrumental in drawing up the first set of goals and in pointing out the general areas most seriously in need of attention by a civic policy group such as the mayor's committee. During the committee's first two years, these researchers formed part of its central core of "prime movers." Other prime movers included the mayor himself, a social worker, a small businessman, and a leader in the Negro community. All the prime movers were relatively free of sanctions; two or three were exceptionally skilled in interpersonal relations; most could devote considerable time to committee activities; and several, including the two prime movers who were Negro, were well versed in effective strategy and tactics. But this "inner circle" did suffer seriously from the absence of a prime mover close to the center of Valleytown's economic power structure, a fact that probably explains much of its failure to progress effectively in the area of industrial employment of Negroes.

THE OIL CITY INTERGROUP COUNCIL

Oil City is a southwestern community that experienced sudden growth during World War II as a result of the rapid expansion of three industries: oil, cotton growing, and corporate fruit and vegetable farming. The city is located in a state whose intergroup relations patterns and attitudes are generally more northern than southern. But when cotton growing and oil migrated from the deep South and other sections of the Southwest, there was an influx into Oil City of large numbers of white and Negro people whose intergroup attitudes and behavior patterns were southern. Other southern influences long present in Oil City came from a large group of white residents who had migrated from the border-south dustbowl area during the early and middle 1930's. The result was a peculiar mixture of conflicting intergroup practices and attitudes: the public schools were integrated, except where residential segregation, which was great, created predominantly white or predominantly Negro grade schools (the city's one public high school was integrated); the state had a civil-rights statute prohibiting discrimination in public places, but it was honored mainly in the breach; Negroes, barred from employment in most industries, notably oil, were limited almost entirely to the cotton fields and menial railroad and construction labor.

Oil City's ethnic picture was further complicated by the presence of large numbers of Filipinos and Mexican nationals (many of them "wetbacks," illegally in this country), who worked the fruit and vegetable crops. There was also a relatively stable Mexican-American population, employed mainly in railroading and fruit and vegetable farming, plus a small group of Japanese and Chinese Americans who worked as gardeners, grocers, and restaurant owners. Except for the middle-class Japanese and Chinese Americans, all of Oil City's racial and nationality groups were overwhelmingly of the working and lower classes, many of them migrant farm laborers living at a bare subsistence level.

Oil City's intergroup relations problems were numerous and ranged in severity from the subsistence economy of Negro and Mexican migrants to the social isolation of the two oriental groups. There was a clear need for a city-wide policy organization that could work toward enforcement of laws already on the statute books and establishment of fair policy in areas where policy was ambiguous or discriminatory.

Early in 1950, a small group of motivated people, feeling strongly the city's need for an intergroup action organization, organized the Oil City Intergroup Council. From the beginning, the organization was entirely private, with no formal or informal official status; its members never considered working toward the formation of a mayor's commission and voted against affiliating with a state-wide intergroup action organization. Participation was poor from the first, in both numbers and breadth of occupational, ethnic, and community leadership representation. The methods it chose to use exclusively were public exhortation and private negotiation, with emphasis on the former. But since the council made only one minor and unsuccessful attempt to involve key community leaders in its program, reliance on these methods proved equally unsuccessful. As an action organization, then, the Oil City Intergroup Council was neither fish nor fowl. It was not a private militant organization like the NAACP, fighting segregation and discriminaton through the courts; nor was it a negotiating organization having the prestige of either city officialdom or key community leadership behind it. It is doubtful that many more than its own forty or fifty members even knew of its existence.

Schoolteachers and clergymen predominated among the intergroup council's prime movers. These people were highly motivated and utterly sincere. But their efforts were hampered because they lacked time, they lacked intergroup relations experience or training, and they lacked the kind of prestige that could be expected to influence Oil City's most important gatekeepers. Ethnic representation was narrow and not very representative. The single Mexican-American board member was a housewife and church worker whose contacts with the Mexican-American community were severely limited by the fact that she was not Catholic. There were two Negro board members, one a clergyman, the other a retired beautician; both were more interested in the local NAACP branch than in the intergroup council. Two Jewish rabbis, the most active of whom ultimately left the city, and a few representatives of the oriental groups rounded out the board's ethnic membership.

In addition to the prime movers' lack of time, experience, and community-wide prestige, most of them were highly vulnerable to sanctions. One Oil City minister had been forced to leave the community by parishioners who disliked his intergroup relations activity. Two schoolteachers had been reprimanded because they did not expressly forbid interracial dancing at a high-school party. All were aware that they could lose either their jobs or their limited influence if they pushed their individual or collective action efforts "too far."

As a result of these inadequacies, the Oil City Intergroup Council was never much more than a discussion group. This, of course, was its major failure as an action organization. Three or four of its board members did manage to persuade the board of education to hire a Negro teacher for one of the grade schools. But this was not the accomplishment it might seem, since the school's student body was all Negro, and the principal was very much in favor of hiring Negro teachers. Some of the council's schoolteacher members organized a high-school interracial club. This group engineered a successful boycott of a small restaurant and student "hangout" whose owner refused to serve Negro students. Later, the interracial club, with adult guidance, persuaded the city council to enact a municipal ordinance prohibiting the use of discriminatory signs in establishments serving the public. These were important achievements, but peripheral to the intergroup council itself. As an action organization, the council was largely ineffective, although it did provide a forum for discussion that probably reinforced the fair-play sentiments of its members.

THE TOURISTVILLE COUNCIL FOR UNITY

The Touristville Council for Unity is one of two branches of a state-wide intergroup action organization that came into being shortly after World War II, largely through the efforts of one man. Branches were organized in the state's two leading cities, working separately on purely local matters and pooling resources for projects of state-wide importance. Both branches were vigorous and effective; the Touristville branch is discussed here because it was the first organized, the largest, and the state organization's full-time executive was located in Touristville.

The council was organized initially by a physician, well known and respected throughout the state, who retired from practice in order to devote full time to improving intergroup relations. Before making any organizational moves, he consulted with a university professor, one of the country's leading intergroup relations authorities. This man advised the retired doctor to organize a city-wide and ultimately a state-wide action group that would be representative of ethnic groups, the motivated majority, and as many key community leaders as the group could involve. There was no problem of initial financing, since the doctor had set aside a substantial sum of his own money to invest in intergroup relations work.

The Touristville Council for Unity got off to an auspicious start. At the doctor's urging, a number of important community leaders agreed to serve on the board of directors, and a few of them were genuinely and continuously active. To increase the support of community leaders, special "advisory boards" were formed for those people who did not wish to participate actively but were willing to lend their names to the letterhead and donate money. As a fundraiser, the doctor-founder of the council was without parallel, and the organization was able to support a full-time executive from the beginning.

Minority participation on the Touristville council was not so broad as council leaders would have liked. The Jewish community was well represented, and there were several well-educated and highly motivated young Negroes active in the organization. But the official leaders of the NAACP and Urban League usually participated in name only, partly because the key NAACP leaders felt the council was usurping territory that belonged to their own organization. (However, the two groups were able to collaborate effectively on one major project, to be discussed later, that put both organizations "on the map" in that region.) The council's major participation gap was the absence of members of the region's three other important groups—Mexican Americans, Indians, and Orientals.

The council's prime movers were a knowledgeable and effective group. The principal figure was the retired doctor, invaluable because of his personal prestige, his fund-raising ability, his high motivation, and the fact that he could devote virtually full time and effort to the council. The second most vital prime mover was the paid executive, a young man with energy and skill in interpersonal relations, who had been trained under the university professor with whom the doctor-founder first consulted. The others included a young attorney from an old, respected family, a free-lance writer with a number of important newspaper and magazine contacts, the director of a large social agency, a Jewish Community Center executive, two or three college and public school teachers, and a woman who formerly wrote for the Negro press.

The Council for Unity undertook a large number of different projects and used a wide variety of methods, on the theory that discrimination and segregation should be attacked directly and wherever they appeared in the fabric of community life. The council's program faced severe handicaps in the absence of any state civil-rights or fair employment practices legislation. In addition, the school laws made high-school segregation optional and grade-school segregation mandatory, with the result that the great majority of the schools throughout the state were segregated even where segregation was optional. Nevertheless, the council used what tools were available, and to good effect. Among the organization's accomplishments for the first five years were the following:

1. Touristville had a little-known ordinance prohibiting discrimination on city-owned property. Council leaders pointed this out to city officials, with the result that a large motion-picture theater, located on city property, dropped its policy of segregated seating, and the restaurant at the municipal airport abandoned its policy of not serving Negroes.

2. Two small communities near Touristville were segregating their Negro school children into a badly dilapidated former dance hall, exactly halfway between the two towns. Not only were the Negro children receiving seriously inadequate schooling, but taxpayers were spending several hundred dollars per pupil per year in order to finance this segregation (three times the yearly cost of educating white children in the two communities). Council leaders combined publicity and negotiation to change this situation. Using principally an economic argument, they appealed to school officials

personally and to the public in the form of a widely circulated pamphlet describing this specific school situation in all its inadequacy and unfairness. The approach worked. The all-Negro school was closed, and the students absorbed into the schools in their respective communities.

3. Again using a judicious mixture of publicity and negotiation, the council was able to bring about the abandonment of a discriminatory policy in a cemetery for war veterans (see chap. 9, p. 171, for details of this case).

4. Unquestionably, the council's greatest achievement was the part it played, together with the NAACP and other individuals and groups, in changing the school laws in the state. The council's doctor-founder and paid executive spent weeks lobbying in the state legislature for a law that would end school segregation in the state. Lawyer members of the council drafted a proposed bill, then continued to work revising the bill as the legislative hearings continued. Council leaders raised funds to support this lobbying activity and organized a grass-roots postcard campaign to bring additional pressure to bear on the legislators. They talked with school officials to get their ideas on desegregation—how it could be brought about, whether it would work. The result was passage by the legislature of a bill that made all segregation optional; it was no longer mandatory to segregate grade-school children, and the decision whether or not to do so was left to the boards of the various school districts. The council had worked for a stronger law, but even this one proved effective. The board of education in the state's other leading city voted to desegregate immediately, and most of the smaller communities followed. Then, following a court case prepared by the Council for Unity and the NAACP, the Touristville Board of Education voted to discontinue segregation in the schools.

Following the successful school desegregation campaign, the Touristville Council for Unity went into a decline, for reasons having chiefly to do with a change in paid executives. The first executive left for a new job, and a young woman was hired to replace him. She was motivated and well trained in intergroup relations, but in her interpersonal relations not as skilled as her predecessor. She tended to take policy-making and negotiations into her own hands, using the board chiefly as a clearing-house. As a result, when a controversial action was taken, the more conservative and influential board members and supporters of the organization, feeling they had had little part in the decision-making process, began to fall away. Most of them ultimately withdrew, leaving the council with only its hard core of motivated liberals. And, finally, a rift developed between this executive and the council's doctor-founder, causing him to resign as the organization's chief fund-raiser. Having no assurance of a continuing income, the board decided to dispense with a paid executive, at least temporarily, and to spend the next few months in re-evaluation and program-planning.

The differences among these organizations can be high-lighted by comparing them directly, on the criteria of effectiveness, in Table 11. By this kind of semisystematic appraisal of the action organizations in a community, a practitioner can determine more easily which of them he will work with and, for those he does work with, perhaps gain a clearer understanding of how his participation can help to strengthen them and make them more effective.

b) Establishing Working Relationships with Action Organizations

Assuming, now, that an intergroup relations practitioner has appraised the status of intergroup activity in his community, how does he establish the most effective working relationship with action organizations? This depends considerably on the amount of time and effort he can devote to it.

If he is burdened with the hundred-and-one duties of an on-going program in an organization whose prime objective is not intergroup relations, then it may be largely spare-time activity. But even in the absence of time, there are some important things he can do. He can, at least, become a member of those action organizations he considers worth while and can contribute as generously as his means permit. Effective action organizations require financial aid. In return for membership contributions in these organizations, the practitioner will receive many different kinds of literature that will help keep him informed on the current status of intergroup relations not only in his own community but also frequently on the state and national levels as well. If he is a person of some standing in the community, he can give his name to causes, even if he cannot give these projects leadership.

If a practitioner has a little time to devote to intergroup re-

TABLE 11

Comparison of Three Action Organizations According to
Certain Criteria of Effectiveness

	Valleytown Mayor's Committee	Oil City Intergroup Council	Touristville Council for Unity
Organizational structure:			
Official or unofficial?	Official	Unofficial	Unofficial
Autonomous or affiliated?	Autonomous	Autonomous	Affiliated
Concern with intergroup relations?	Primary	Primary	Primary
Source of funds?	Local organizations	Memberships	Big donors and memberships
Participation:			
Influential leaders?	A few	None	Several
Lawyers?	None	None	Several
Minority representatives?	Uneven	Not strong	Sophisticated and motivated
Labor?	One	None	Several
Other?	Social work and miscellaneous	Largely clergy and teachers	Schoolteachers and social workers
Effectiveness of prime movers:			
Time and effort?	Good	Poor	Excellent
Motivation?	Good	Good	Good

TABLE 11—*Continued*

	Valleytown Mayor's Committee	Oil City Intergroup Council	Touristville Council for Unity
Interpersonal effectiveness?	Uneven	Not strong	Good in early stages, but several changes for the worse
Understanding of strategy and tactics?	Not strong	Weak	Good
Freedom from sanctions?	Uneven	Poor	Good
Major accomplishments: Proposing legislation	.....	Ordinance prohibiting discriminatory signs (collaborative)	Permissive desegregation of schools bill passed; civil-rights bill introduced
Establishing fair-play policies By direct negotiation	Negro schoolteacher; integrated housing projects; Negro telephone operator; a few individual grievances	.....	Desegregation of one theater and airport restaurant; several inferior or Negro schools desegregated; abolition of discriminatory veterans' burial policy; desegregation of Negro draftees

TABLE 11—*Continued*

	Valleytown Mayor's Committee	Oil City Intergroup Council	Touristville Council for Unity
By indirect or collaborative efforts	Negro member of service club; Negro representative on settlement house board; Negro visiting nurse hired	Negro schoolteacher; student restaurant	Desegregation of the high schools
Establishing favorable atmosphere	Workshop for group workers on intergroup relations	Brotherhood Week festival	Collaboration in a number of workshops, institutes, and conferences
Major failures in negotiation	Negotiation with prefabricating plant; negotiation with bus company; negotiation for Negro over-the-counter salespersons	. . . .	Housing project segregation

154

lations, how can he most effectively use it? Perhaps the best thing for him to do would be to utilize his special talents to greatest advantage in the intergroup relations action field. For example, a lawyer could volunteer to be legal adviser to the local NAACP or some other intergroup action organization. A teacher might suggest to his principal that he appoint an intergroup relations committee to consider how the most progressive thinking in intergroup relations could be incorporated into the school curriculum; this suggestion might then result in the formation of a city-wide workshop for teachers during the summer. A group worker—say, the director of the YWCA branch—could propose to the Council of Social Agencies that an intergroup relations committee be appointed to see how the youth or group-work sections of the council might adopt better intergroup practices in the group-work field.

In each of these examples, the practitioner may not have the time to do the bulk of the work. He *can* be alert and make suggestions that will benefit the action organizations, because of his special talents or any special knowledge or understanding he has of the structure and functioning of his community.

If a practitioner has a more substantial amount of time, he can contribute by being a working member of the committees and boards of the organizations he considers to be most effective. Organizations run by a competent professional, who stays in the background and does not try to "do it all himself," get the bulk of their work done through special committees. As pointed out earlier, the professional needs lay board members to work with him on action projects. This, of course, is in addition to being a member of other organizations in the field.

If a practitioner has a considerable amount of time to devote to intergroup relations, he will want to participate in the way that is most rewarding: by being a prime mover of an effective organization. His achievements in this area need be limited only by his qualifications. These have been elaborated above.

c) Implementing New Organizational Forms

The practitioner who works with several different organizations devoted to action in intergroup relations should bear in mind that each may use appropriate, quite different action techniques. There is not necessarily one "right" way to proceed; what might be appropriate for one organization might be quite inappropriate for another.

The organization with few sanctions on its militancy may use the more controversial methods of publicity and mass demonstration. The more moderate organizations might restrict themselves to negotiation. Actually, different organizations working in different ways for the same objective may be one of the most effective city-wide strategies. The "needling" of violators by the more militant organizations may make it possible for the negotiators to accomplish an objective that otherwise would have been difficult. If success occurs, everyone will want to take credit, and everyone should be given credit. Since the co-ordination of action efforts in this way is good community-wide strategy, many communities feel the need of some co-ordinating machinery to make sure that the left hand knows what the right hand is doing. Sometimes this will require a new co-ordinating committee; sometimes existing organizational forms can be used.

The co-ordinating group should probably comprise the prime movers of the most effective action organizations in the community. Just as the professional will operate mostly out of the limelight in his own bailiwick, so this group will operate largely behind the scenes in planning the main lines of strategy for given objectives. If the key professionals can establish effective relationships among themselves, they can be the core of a really successful community-wide program.

CHAPTER 9

The Strategy of Negotiating
for Change

In an intergroup relations action program a major aim is to
get key leaders in various sectors of community life involved
in the planning and execution of the changes needed to obtain
the action objectives. But this is not always possible. Some key
individuals are not interested in the action objectives of local
intergroup relations leaders and may even oppose them. We
call individuals who, because of their strategic positions, might
widen the participation of minorities in a sector of community life, but are unwilling to do so, "reluctant gatekeepers."
They are the school superintendents who can hire Negro teachers or refuse them; the personnel men who can place Negroes
in white-collar positions or close the doors to them; the mortgage bankers or real estate agents who can pave the way for
Negroes to find decent housing or stand in their way.

The most effective way to work with reluctant gatekeepers
is through negotiation backed up by sanctions. The basic strategy of successful negotiation is the use of leverage. By this, we
mean the ability to show reluctant gatekeepers that the consequences of not changing their intergroup practices are less
desirable than the consequences of changing them. If, for example, an employer becomes convinced that the adverse publicity he will get by continuing to discriminate will be more
distasteful than the possibility of a few of his employees' objecting to his hiring Negroes, then leverage has been successfully used. The basic strategy of negotiation, then, has two
facets: (1) interpreting the consequences of change as *less*
threatening than the reluctant gatekeepers suppose and (2)

interpreting the consequences of not changing the practices as *more* threatening by bringing negative sanctions to bear. We maximize the leverage in the situation by having the gatekeeper weigh the consequences of these two courses of action and by widening the gap between them as much as possible.

Working toward a More Realistic Evaluation of the Consequences of Change

Most reluctant gatekeepers tend to exaggerate the negative consequences of change in intergroup relations. Much of the success in negotiation depends on convincing the gatekeeper that a transition to better intergroup practices can be made smoothly and without trouble. There are several ways to bring the gatekeeper to a more realistic evaluation of what is likely to happen. Negotiators can point out this important principle:

PROPOSITION 24: *Where there are clear lines of authority or administrative control, people tend to go along with the rules and regulations that are passed down from the top, even when their initial feelings about these regulations may not be favorable.*

Employers often object strongly to "coercing" their employees into accepting new intergroup practices. This sudden solicitude for employees' feelings is often ironic, in the light of a host of other distasteful or restrictive rules and regulations that the employer enforces daily and never sees as "coercive."

In the absence of administrative controls, where free-choosing patrons or customers are involved, experience shows that the patronage will go along with new intergroup practices as long as the basic services or products are not altered. If a department store introduces a policy of hiring Negro salesgirls, without fanfare, many patrons won't even notice the change or will think it has always been that way. And since the quality of the merchandise remains the same, even the objectors will continue to patronize the store, since for most customers the merchandise, not the sales personnel, is the primary consideration.

Reluctant gatekeepers sometimes state that they wouldn't mind serving Negro customers or hiring Negro secretarial help, if other firms would do the same; but they don't see why they alone should jeopardize their business by instituting something as controversial as this. We have found a number of instances that suggest that this "If-I'm-the-only-one-it-will-hurt-me" principle does not hold up. A state-wide firm with progressive intergroup policies decided that these policies should be put into practice in a southern border community where such things were unheard of. Restrictions to colored trade were removed, and the company continued to do a thriving business with a mixed clientele. A fashionable cafeteria in a southwestern city we visited served Negroes while other restaurants serving similar clientele refused them; waiting lines of customers attested to the continued popularity of this establishment. In this same city, one of the department stores employed a Negro salesman in the men's department without loss of patronage. Frequently, intergroup relations policy of this sort will increase the patronage of an establishment because of favorable reaction in the Negro community and among other persons favoring democratic practices.

It is helpful in bringing reluctant gatekeepers to a more realistic evaluation of the consequences of changing their intergroup practices to have available for negotiation meetings illustrations of "success experiences" of similar establishments. Where several gatekeepers in a specific sector of community life have integrated practices that have proved successful, their experiences should be used as illustrations to help convert their colleagues. The reluctant gatekeeper may well hold his fellow-gatekeepers in higher esteem than people in the intergroup action field, whom he may consider radical or "long-haired" or unrealistic. Furthermore, the experience of his colleagues is convincing proof that integration is possible in his own area of activity. And his colleagues will have had experience in the actual details of accomplishing integration that may be useful if passed along to him.

In the absence of colleagues in the same community who have integrated practices, help can sometimes be found in the experiences of gatekeepers in other communities in the same part of the country. For example, if the hospitals in a community were reluctant to employ Negro nurses, the successful experiences of a hospital or two in a near-by community that had done so would give the negotiators leverage in answering such objections as "We're not ready for it here." It would probably be possible for the negotiators to persuade the hospital administrators from a near-by community to sit in on the negotiation meetings to give personal testimony on the success of their change in practices.

Negotiators should point out to reluctant gatekeepers how unwarranted exaggerated fears of trouble are. If firmness, not vacillation, characterizes a transition to new practices, the vast bulk of intergroup experience shows that within a short time the new practices will be thoroughly taken for granted. In some situations, gatekeepers can be persuaded to give new intergroup practices a "trial run" to assure themselves that the consequences will not be disruptive. If a trial run is made, however, it should be undertaken in good faith, with the intention of making it permanent if it succeeds. The gatekeeper should not, for instance, sound out customers or employees by telling them, "We're just trying this thing out, what's your reaction?" An important principle here is:

PROPOSITION 25: *Polling those involved in advance of an intergroup change typically calls forth many more negative reactions than will actually occur if the change is undertaken as matter-of-factly as any other change that might be instituted.*

The negotiators can point out to the reluctant gatekeeper that even if a few individuals object strenuously, the fact that the vast majority will go along with better intergroup relations is more important. Even if an employee or two quit or a customer is lost, democratic principles will have been established; new customers will replace the old, and the talents of minority persons will be utilized in keeping with their skills and abilities rather than wasted in support of an outmoded bigotry.

To sum up: the negotiator tries to mobilize the reassuring experiences of good intergroup relations practice and to convince the reluctant gatekeeper that he can change the intergroup relations practices without fear of trouble.

Making Effective Use of Negative Sanctions

Actually, we know little of what brings about the success of one negotiation attempt and leads to the failure of another. Fortuitous circumstances are frequently extremely important; the personalities of the individuals involved may be crucial. But a few rules of thumb can be suggested that may be helpful. There is perhaps one basic principle:

PROPOSITION 26: *Negotiations for intergroup change are more frequently successful if the sanctions that can be brought to bear on the key gatekeepers are thoughtfully evaluated and an approach used that maximizes the leverage these sanctions afford.*

Negative sanctions, like the use of unfavorable publicity or court action, are frequently unpleasant, embarrassing, or even damaging to reluctant gatekeepers. Otherwise, they would not be effective sanctions. But a public spirited or progressive intergroup relations leader does not want to be punitive; he wants to work in a friendly, co-operative way to establish better intergroup relations practices. The punitive use of negative sanctions may create hard feelings and make impossible subsequent co-operation in establishing a smooth transition to better practices. The skilful practitioner tries not to invoke negative sanctions until all alternatives in negotiation are exhausted. But he can make effective use of negative sanctions in the negotiation process. To do this, the negotiator makes clear what negative sanctions there are that can be brought to bear. He indicates his firm intention to use these sanctions if a satisfactory solution cannot be worked out by negotiation. But he also makes quite clear his great reluctance to use them unless forced to do so because no satisfactory arrangements can be worked out.

The negotiator's success in making effective use of negative sanctions requires great skill in interpersonal relations. We have the impression that the use of sanctions in negotiation is seldom successful if the negotiators are hostile and use the sanctions as a threat to the gatekeeper, e.g., "You do what we want, or else you'll get what's coming to you!" The tone of negotiation should be friendly and firm. Used in this way, negative sanctions add immensely to the leverage of the negotiator. The effectiveness of negative sanctions, of course, varies, depending upon whether they are legal, economic, or moral.

Legal Sanctions

By "legal sanctions" we mean legislation enacted in support of fair employment practices, civil rights, and other fair-play practices that can be legally enforced. We can distinguish two varieties: (a) legal sanctions where the enacting body has provided enforcement commissions that can bring about compliance by negotiation, resorting to court action only if negotiation fails, and (b) legislation that provides redress only through court action. Most fair employment practices legislation provides for enforcement commissions. In some states it is mandatory for a state commission to do everything it can by negotiation before considering legal action. Thus these states have a skilled staff of negotiators who have accumulated experience and wisdom in bringing about smooth transitions to better intergroup practices. In their hands, legal sanctions become a powerful educational device.

Many people see civil-rights and fair employment practices legislation as compulsory or punitive. They say laws are not good because you can't legislate away people's prejudices. They feel that the only thing we can do is educate reluctant gatekeepers into more enlightened practices. But, as many intergroup relations practitioners now realize, although we may not be able to legislate away prejudices, we certainly can make it inconvenient for gatekeepers to put their prejudices into practice. The function of these enforcement commissions is to make perfectly clear that continued defiance of the law will have unpleasant consequences for the violator and, at the same time, to convince the violator that a change in practices will not have consequences as dire as he anticipates.

Enforcement commissions backed up by legal sanctions represent negotiation at its best, because the commission is in a position to exert maximum leverage. Under these circumstances, the education of the gatekeeper proceeds apace. It is assured because of the position in which he finds himself. He is faced with actual penalties if he refuses to listen. He is personally, often economically, involved. It is direct person-to-person education. He and his firm are in the undesirable moral position of violating a law of the land based on the high principle of fair play. Where individual grievances are brought to the attention of local intergroup relations leaders, they should encourage the aggrieved individual to bring the matter to the attention of any enforcement commission that may have jurisdiction in that area of community life.

Where there is no enforcement commission, legal sanctions can still be used to strengthen local negotiators in bringing about compliance with the law. Even though a local organization, such as a hotel or restaurant, has clearly violated a state law referring to public accommodations, local intergroup leaders should make every effort to bring about a change in policy and practice by negotiation before considering redress by court action. But, in the negotiations, they should make clear that court action is their only alternative if the violator does not change.

Occasionally, where a stubborn gatekeeper refuses to comply with the law, a court case can serve a valuable function in helping to establish fair-play practices in the community at large. Other gatekeepers in the same line of business in the community rapidly learn of the violator's unhappy experiences in being brought into court on the embarrassing charge of discrimination. Fearing the same legal consequences themselves, they are more likely to abide by the law when next faced with a similar circumstance.

The important thing to bear in mind in invoking legal sanctions such as court action is that the objective is not merely to acquire for the aggrieved individual a few hundred dollars in penalty fines; the intergroup objective is to establish fair practices for the future, not only for the violating firm but also for firms in a similar line of endeavor. Thus an important objective would be a declaration by the top authorities in the organization, stating that they intend to see the law enforced in the future and that they want all members of the staff involved with it to see that their day-to-day practices conform to the law. In a chain of restaurants, for instance, top management would notify each of the restaurant managers of their intention to comply with the law in the future. Managers would then be requested to inform all waiters and waitresses of this policy. It would also be desirable if the trade association representing restaurant and tavern keepers could be urged to issue a statement to all its members, saying something to the effect that, in the light of the recent court case and its unpleasantness, the association is urging all its members to notify their personnel directly involved in serving the public that they expect complete co-operation in complying with the law.

Economic Sanctions

Economic sanctions that bring direct financial pressure to bear on gatekeepers give the negotiator important points of leverage also. Perhaps the most common of these is the customer boycott. Wherever a substantial number of customers can be persuaded to drop their patronage of a given firm until it changes its practices, the reluctant gatekeeper can be convinced that the consequences of not changing his practices are rather serious. The problem is how to persuade enough customers to apply this pressure. Picketing is sometimes an effective way of enforcing a boycott, as the following incident illustrates:

The union-management contract at a steel mill in a border town provided that men working overtime receive meal tickets good at any restaurant in the plant vicinity. At one time, several Negroes, taking advantage of this plan, were refused service in some of the near-by eating places. The Negro workers immediately informed the union of this. The union picketed the offending restaurants. According to the union president, "We didn't have to picket more than ten minutes" before the restaurant capitulated. Now all of the restaurants near the mill honor the meal tickets of Negro workers.

Many people appear to be reluctant to go on a picket line and "make a spectacle of themselves." But they should remember that many people hesitate to cross a picket line, and with some it is a matter of profound conviction. Picketing can be quite effective in communities or neighborhoods where such thinking is widespread.

Organizational support can sometimes be elicited to enforce a boycott. An intergroup relations committee might ask its members not to patronize certain establishments and to favor others. Negro organizations in border cities with large Negro populations might ask their members not to patronize certain department stores that refuse to hire or upgrade Negroes. We know that it is difficult to modify the behavior of large numbers of customers through boycott requests of this sort; however, the possibility of making such requests is useful to the negotiator in increasing his leverage in meetings with the reluctant gatekeepers. This is because the reluctant gatekeeper does not know how effective the negotiators might be in organizing a boycott; he deplores the loss of even a single customer; and he does not like the idea of his firm being widely talked about in unfavorable terms.

Another technique that has sometimes been used successfully to enforce a boycott is the sitdown. The following case illustrates the potential power of a sitdown:

In one community a group of young people, both white and Negro, wanted to bring about a change in the practices of a drugstore that did not serve Negroes. As regular patrons vacated the soda fountain counter, they took seats. When the Negroes were refused service, they continued to sit there as a group and thus tied up the entire counter.

After some futile attempts to get the sitdowners out, the drugstore owner got in touch with his attorney. The attorney, who happened by chance to be a board member of a local intergroup relations organization, immediately arranged for a negotiation session between the leaders of the sitdown group and the manager. In the negotiation sessions, the manager became convinced that he should try a policy of serving Negroes for a month. He said that he would discontinue the practice if anything troublesome happened. Subsequently, he did start serving Negroes, nothing happened, and the practice of serving Negroes became well established.

Militant tactics like this often precipitate negotiation sessions where the reluctant gatekeepers are really prepared to negotiate because they have already felt the impact of negative sanctions. It should be pointed out that using negative sanctions prior to negotiation does risk incurring the antagonism of the gatekeeper and may make genuine negotiation more difficult.

One of the most effective of economic sanctions to get movement from employers is the labor union's use of the strike threat in contract negotiations. Where unions incorporate into their demands contract clauses that require fair-play practices in hiring and upgrading, all the economic pressure that grows from the union's strength can be brought to bear on reluctant gatekeepers. All the major unions of the country have fairly explicit policies on intergroup relations practices, but these are not always effectively implemented at the local level, and many union leaders are themselves reluctant gatekeepers. Negotiation with local union leaders must be initiated if they are reluctant to work for fair employment practices. If, however, there is fairly widespread apathy among union leaders about intergroup relations matters, perhaps a new committee is called for, such as a city-wide labor committee for fair employment practices. This committee would hope to involve the key union leaders in the process of discovering and deciding for themselves that the economic sanctions of their unions should be used more effectively with employers to obtain fair employment practices.

Another economic sanction that is rare but effective where available is "control of the purse-strings." Several examples illustrate this sanction. Certain school systems in southern Illinois practiced segregation in violation of state ordinances. Since the state educational authorities were instructed not to make state funds available to schools whose administrative practices were not in line with state law, the state administration could apply considerable pressure on local school systems to change their discriminatory practices. In cases of license renewal, the license-issuing board may be prevailed upon to cut off the source of income of licensees who violate state civil-rights legislation. For example, a liquor license-issuing board might suspend the license of a tavern keeper who did not live up to state civil-rights legislation requiring that people be served regardless of race, creed, or national origin.

Sometimes economic sanctions can be brought to bear through the control of governmental purchasing power or contract negotiation. If the policy can be established that a governmental body that raises its funds by taxation of *all* the people should not allocate its funds to organizations that discriminate against segments of the population, then government administrators may be prevailed upon to purchase only from firms that do not discriminate. The President's Committee on Government Contracts operates in this way, since federal contracts are not supposed to be given to firms that discriminate. And there is every reason for a state or even a municipal government to scrutinize its list of customers to make sure that they measure up with regard to fair practices.

Moral Sanctions

By "moral sanctions" we mean the bringing of social disapproval to bear on gatekeepers who are reluctant to live up to the American Creed standards of the community. Social disapproval can be brought to bear through the negotiators themselves, through colleagues of the gatekeeper who are willing to co-operate, or through publicity directed to the general public.

A straight appeal to the moral rightness of fair play is not always ineffective. Sometimes people *can* be persuaded to change their practices just because discrimination and segregation are "wrong." We encountered a courageous school administrator from a southwestern city who was able to win his board over to desegregation by a direct appeal to its moral rightness. Because a sense of rightness is attached to fair-play objectives, objections to the moral argument are usually raised on practical grounds: "This isn't the time to do it," "We can't move too quickly in these matters," "We're just heading for trouble if we try and change that," and so on. The basic principle in this kind of negotiation is:

PROPOSITION 27: *Get a reluctant gatekeeper on record in favor of fair-play practices, and he will generally have difficulty evading this commitment later without calling forth social disapproval.*

There is a major point of strategy to be borne in mind in doing this: the negotiator should try to foresee all possible evasions that the reluctant gatekeeper might introduce to justify his not living up to the fair-play point of view he expressed.

For example, suppose that an action group is negotiating with an employer to hire Negroes, and the gatekeeper is reluctant. In the first meetings with the gatekeeper, the negotiators state their objective in seeing that Negroes have better employment opportunities and attempt to get the reluctant gatekeeper on record as saying he is not against hiring Negroes in his own firm. After getting such a statement from the gatekeeper, the negotiators then ask him whether or not the firm does employ Negroes. Assuming that the gatekeeper says No, the negotiators ask why that is. If the answer is that the Negroes who apply are not qualified, the negotiators follow through and discover in detail just what qualifications are necessary. They talk with the personnel man to make sure of mutual understanding about these qualifications. They contact candidates in the Negro community who meet the stated requirements. Instead of just sending these candidates to the firm on their own, the negotiators apply additional pressure by calling the personnel man, telling him that these applicants are coming in, and elaborating their reasons for thinking they are well qualified.

After a series of preparatory steps of this sort have been taken to insure no slip-up, it is difficult for the gatekeeper to refuse to hire Negroes. If he does refuse, he has to go back on his word and must risk the social disapproval that goes with "being a welcher." In cases such as this, the task of the negotiator is getting the gatekeeper on record in favor of fair-play practices; and this is not always easy, as the following case illustrates:

Following a Brotherhood Week meeting in a midwestern community, a small group of people interested in intergroup relations decided to negotiate with the largest employer in town to try to get the plant to hire Negroes. An interracial committee met with the owner of the plant and two personnel men. One member of the original group—an "elder statesman" in the community—would not take part in the negotiations because he felt that the presence of Negroes would inhibit forthright answers. The chief spokesman of the committee stated the purpose of the visit in inoffensive, general terms; others on the committee raised questions which became increasingly specific. The company men evaded the questions, refusing to state their policy clearly, merely reiterating that Negroes must fill out applications which would then be considered along with others. They said that all employees must be qualified and that, to their knowledge, no Negroes were. Even when the company men were confronted with the fact that one of the Negro committee members (a qualified worker in the trade with experience in two near-by cities) had applied for a job at the plant and been refused, the company men evaded the issue, saying, "Well, then, your application was considered with the rest." Despite further efforts by committee members, the company men refused to state a definite policy with regard to hiring Negroes. There the matter rested.

This group's failure to wring a positive policy statement from the plant management can probably be best explained by the fact that the group had no majority-group members whose standing in the community could be expected to influence plant policy. It is true that this state had no fair employment practices legislation, but this is by no means a fatal handicap where other powerful sanctions are available to negotiators for change. In this instance, direct economic sanctions were also lacking, since the plant was absentee-owned and its market was nation-wide, not merely local. In addition, the union in the plant had leadership that was indifferent to the problem and could not be expected to fight for a fair practices clause in the union-management contract. Hence the necessity for bringing moral sanctions to bear through exerting meaningful pressure from the community. In this case, the group's strategy was good: to put the gatekeeper on record as favoring fair employment practices, as a first step to the eventual employment of Negroes. The failure lay in the absence of key community leaders who could effectively implement this strategy. The group might have been better advised to sacrifice an interracial committee composition for this first negotiation, in order to retain the services of the one motivated "elder statesman" they had.

Where a reluctant gatekeeper is really a "hold-out" in a community setting where most of his colleagues have good intergroup practices, the mobilization of their moral disapproval may bring him around. Suppose that all but two of the movie theaters in a community have integrated seating for Negroes and whites. Intergroup relations leaders might organize a meeting of all the movie managers to share their experiences and discuss how the remaining vestiges of segregation could be removed. At this meeting, the managers of the integrated theaters could probably answer any objections the reluctant two might raise, and it might become painfully evident to all that these objections were just evasions to avoid adopting nonsegregated practices. The reluctant two would probably sense the disapproval felt by the others; some of the others might overtly express it. Under these circumstances, a reluctant gatekeeper might be persuaded to "give it a trial run," especially if he knew that he might avoid the consequences of other negative sanctions, such as an organized boycott or negative publicity.

Because good intergroup relations enjoy the standing of a worth-while moral objective, most gatekeepers prefer not to be known as violators of the moral creed. They will sometimes go to considerable lengths to avoid being publicly accused of discrimination or segregation. This fact puts in the hands of the intergroup relations negotiator one of his most powerful sanctions—negative publicity. Here is a good example:

The only cemetery in a southwestern city that would bury Negroes imposed one restriction on the burial of Negro veterans in the veterans' plot: the next of kin of any Negro veteran wishing to have the body buried there was required to secure notarized letters of permission from the commanding officers of three local veterans' organizations—the American Legion, the Disabled American Veterans, and the Veterans of Foreign Wars. This procedure was clearly discriminatory, since similar letters were not required in the case of white veterans.

Although the city's most prominent intergroup action organization had been assisting Negroes in obtaining this permission, they concluded that by helping to make these arrangements they were implicitly condoning the cemetery's discriminatory practice. Agreeing with this organization that the policy was unnecessary and time-consuming, two of the veterans' groups wrote the cemetery board asking that the procedure be stopped and that all veterans be buried in the plot without regard to race, creed, or color. The issue came to a head two months later when the father of a Negro soldier made application to the cemetery board for his son's burial and was told about having to get the three letters of permission. He went, instead, to the intergroup action organization for help in fighting the cemetery's policy.

Officers of the organization confronted the cemetery board with the two blanket letters and requested that the policy be changed. The board rejected this proposal, but finally agreed to meet with organization members and representatives of the three veterans' groups. At this meeting, the board said that they would *consider* a policy change if the third veterans' group wrote a similar blanket letter. At the next meeting of this group, the chairman failed to bring the matter up. At the next meeting, two members (also members of the intergroup action organization) proposed a resolution which was immediately tabled (again without comment from the chairman). At a third meeting, a member's motion to bring the resolution out for discussion was defeated.

It was then that the intergroup organization decided to release a story to the newspapers. (Such a move had been considered before, but a membership meeting of the organization had voted to postpone such action until after all avenues of negotiation were exhausted.) The story was written by a free-lance writer (also a leader in the intergroup organization), who arranged with the publisher of one of the city's papers to release it under the caption "NO HOME FOR THE BRAVE."

The afternoon the story broke, the "hold-out" veterans' group called an emergency meeting and rapidly passed a resolution asking the cemetery to bury all veterans without regard to race, creed, or color. Two days later, the chairman of the cemetery board released a statement to the effect that a policy change on Negro burials was up to the board and did not hinge on blanket letters from the veterans' organizations. Then the avalanche began: for days, letters to the editor poured in, most of them expressing outrage at the cemetery's policy of discrimination. The outcome was that the cemetery board amended its policy to state that *all* veterans would henceforth be required to have their burial cleared by the veterans' organizations. This is just a formality and a face-saving device; henceforth, white and Negro veterans will be treated alike.

Publicity is most effective as a sanction when the indignities suffered by the person discriminated against most outrage the moral sentiments of the public, as in the veteran's burial case.

It is least successful when it merely confirms the public's and other gatekeepers' impressions that discrimination is standard practice. Much of its value as a sanction lies in gatekeepers' aversion to any kind of publicity which will link them with some kind of fracas or trouble.

Many leaders in intergroup relations settings are reluctant to make effective use of publicity. Perhaps they hesitate to embarrass fellow community leaders; perhaps they are afraid of making enemies. Sometimes they are afraid of antagonizing persons who could impair their business relations or social standing. In actual practice, publicity is probably more often used as a threat than as a reality. Negotiators who use publicity in this way avoid any of these other undesirable consequences; but they must beware that their bluff is not called if they are not prepared to go through with it.

On rare occasions, publicity may actually have a boomerang effect. If the publicity alerts segments of the community that are antagonistic to better intergroup relations and serves as a spur to their organized opposition to the action objective, then it may do more harm than good. But, in an atmosphere of ever improving intergroup relations, persons working for action objectives should keep publicity in mind as a sanction that can be very effective if properly timed.

A final word about the use of sanctions. There is no substitute for forthrightness and courage, both in negotiating for change and in putting new policies into effect. But forthright action sometimes creates tension, and changed practices may precipitate outright conflict. Such contingencies must be foreseen and planned for, and appropriate use made of law-enforcement officers whenever possibilities of overt conflict arise. But intergroup relations leaders should understand that overt intergroup conflict does not arise from using sanctions to bring about a decision to change. Where conflict does arise, it usually comes as a consequence of putting a changed policy into practice, in circumstances where (a) organized opposition or (b)

spontaneous opposition by individuals is permitted by the legitimate authorities to become mob action. It is not the use of sanctions by negotiators for change that produces overt intergroup conflict; it is rather the abdication by the duly constituted authorities of their responsibility to enforce orderly, nonviolent transition, once the change has been decided on.

CHAPTER 10

Continuing Professional Growth

A practitioner cannot expect that by reading this small book he will develop a full set of intergroup relations skills overnight. We do hope that the book points out some of the basic considerations that must be borne in mind by a person hoping to develop his professional skills in intergroup relations. But mature professional skill develops from years of hard work and experience. Because of the setting in which many practitioners find themselves, years may pass with a minimum of professional growth in their capacity for dealing with intergroup relations. Let us look at the personal setting of the practitioner and the difficulties he faces in developing an intergroup relations program.

For one thing, intergroup relations may be peripheral to the main goals of his organization. Unless the practitioner or his board of directors has consciously made good intergroup practices an objective, those connected with the agency may be satisfied with the single fact that they are not having any intergroup relations "trouble." Perhaps their organization includes but one ethnic group or only a token representation of other groups. They may be inclined to say, "We have no problems here." The practitioner in this kind of setting is understandably passive. On the other hand, other experienced persons might feel that the organization is not making use of its intergroup relations opportunities to provide personal growth for the participants in its program.

Second, the practitioner may have a genuinely conservative board to which he is accountable. Because of this, he may be reluctant to come to grips with what board members consider "delicate problems." He may recognize a gap between the professed goals of his organization and actual intergroup relations practices but nevertheless feel uncertain as to what he can do about it without alienating his board.

Third, the practitioner may have difficulty keeping up communication with other professionals in his field. The burdens of a day-to-day program may leave him few opportunities for genuine interchange with practitioners facing similar problems in other organizations. Restricted thus to a local field of vision, he may feel that the intergroup relations problems of his own organization are unique. Even if he recognizes the more general nature of his problems, he may still hesitate to participate in frank discussion about them with other practitioners for fear that he will expose his own program to critical analysis. Frank and open discussion of the shortcomings of one's intergroup relations practices is naturally threatening to the individual practitioner.

Fouth, in any given community there may be no clearly defined professional standards as to what good intergroup relations practices should be. Different organizations have different views of what can be accomplished. The practitioner may have great difficulty in deciding what are realistic goals for his own organization. To some practitioners, gang fights may be merely innocent teen-age exuberance; to others, they represent serious intergroup tensions. To some practitioners, the presence of two or three Negroes in their program will represent successful integration; to others, it signifies only a token gesture. Because few yardsticks have been developed to measure progress in intergroup relations, practitioners may find themselves comfortably ensconced in repeating familiar programs without being analytical about them and in danger of slipping into an unchallenged passivity.

Fifth, practitioners are aware of how sparse our valid knowledge is of just what techniques are most successful in accomplishing intergroup change. They may feel that earnestness, sincerity, and experience are more important than the insights, skills, and procedures that grow out of intergroup training. The practitioner may not think of himself as a conscious expediter of social change.

In a professional setting that has obstacles of this sort, the practitioner who wants to insure his professional growth will work with other professionals to establish standards for intergroup practices in the community, to contribute to the achievement of those standards by his own and other organizations, and to assure the continuing development of his own thinking on intergroup relations. There are several ways that he can do this: (1) If there is a local professional organization for persons in his line of work, he can be an active member of it and can make efforts to see that intergroup relations is a matter of professional concern for the group. (2) In most communities there is a youth, group-work, or recreation division of the Council of Social Agencies. He can work with this organization to see that intergroup objectives are a meaningful part of the division's objectives. (3) He can participate in—perhaps even be instrumental in organizing—community-wide workshops for practitioners in his field. Workshops in intergroup relations have the special advantage of focusing practitioners' attention for at least a day or two exclusively on intergroup relations and what can be done about this area in their own organizations. (4) He can work with other persons trying to promote better intergroup relations in the community at large by supporting and becoming active in whatever intergroup action organizations there are.

By participating actively in the intergroup relations work going on in his community through workshops, his professional association, and other on-going intergroup relations organizations, the practitioner can guarantee his continued professional growth in this field, as he gains new experience and participates in successful action efforts. But, valuable as experience is in giving guidance to intergroup relations practice, in the long run social practice should be based also on scientific knowledge. Genuine professional growth should provide for an expanding horizon of scientific knowledge underlying the professional person's operating skills.

How, then, can the practitioner establish a more effective working relationship with the social scientist? To begin with, the practitioner needs a realistic understanding of what the social scientist can and cannot do. The practitioner frequently does not realize the difficult position he puts the social scientist in when he goes to him for help on specific problem situations he faces in his practice. The social scientist may react in a way that is puzzling to the practitioner. The social scientist may appear overconfident, with a tendency to preach from on high. He may reveal by his remarks that he has an inadequate understanding of what the practitioner already knows. Social scientists frequently fail to recognize how much unformulated knowledge there is currently at work in the practices of "good" practitioners. The social scientist may reveal that he has a very feeble grasp of the relevant factors of which the practitioner has to take account in his day-to-day operations.

Quite often, too, there is a genuine shortage of scientific findings on the things for which the practitioner calls on social science. On top of this, many social scientists are not motivated to make practical applications of their scientific knowledge. In the midst of these kinds of difficulties, the social scientist may be genuinely uncomfortable when confronted with problems of social practice. He is not sure of what he has to offer, and he does not know how to bring what he can offer to bear on the specific problems at hand. Under these circumstances, the practitioner who expects answers from the social scientist is bound to be disappointed.

Needless to say, there are some social scientists who have had field experiences and training that make them sympathetic and understanding of the practitioners' problems. Some practitioners, too, have a clear grasp of what the social scientist is up against and realistically know what they can expect of social research. Under these conditions, collaboration is natural and fruitful.

But, under more usual circumstances, communication will be difficult. The practitioner who then rejects the social scientist is further complicating an already difficult problem in communication, is standing in the way of professional growth that might come to him from collaboration with the social scientist, and is probably overlooking his own blind spots in this matter of social science. The practitioner with the heavy day-to-day activities of an ongoing program may come to the social scientist with a set of predispositions or attitudes that make it difficult for him to co-operate. His perspective on what is good or bad practice may be based on the heavy commitments he has already made in his own progarm. He is under practical pressure to demonstrate short-term concrete results to the policymakers guiding his program.

He may also have a lurking suspicion that some of his intergroup relations practices are not so effective as they might be, and he may hesitate to scrutinize them frankly. He may fear that scientific reflection on specific intergroup practices will bring about doubt as to which of several alternatives is better —a doubt that scientific evidence just cannot resolve at present. Doubts of this sort might immobilize him and make it impossible for him to act decisively in pushing his program forward. He may even harbor real doubts as to whether social science has anything to offer and adopt the attitude "I'll come around when you show me that social science can get results." If any of these thoughts contribute to the practitioner's perception of the social scientist, the problems of communication will be further complicated.

The practitioner's objective in bringing the social scientist into the picture should probably be the establishing of a relationship that is genuinely exploratory for both. If the social scientist does not have answers, he can at least be exploratory as to what the range of answers might be and how some relevant evidence might be obtained. Not getting the answers he wants from the social scientist, the practitioner can at least be exploratory in trying out different intergroup practices to accumulate experience in what works and what does not. If the practitioner has any flexibility in the planning and execution of his program, he and the social scientist may be able to work out a study design that will accumulate significant evidence on certain procedures of social practice. The principles of social action and practice will have to be validated by studying the differential results of different courses of action. Each action effort, each practitioner's technique, each practical field problem, is just a sample of one. Thus adequate quantitative data to show that one course of action is superior to another are difficult for a practitioner to accumulate.

To the practitioner, each concrete problem with which he is faced may appear unique, as indeed it is. But scientific knowledge grows from the standardized accumulation of settings wherein some of the major variables are controlled. Working with an exploratory and experimental perspective will lead to a growth in understanding on the part of both scientist and practitioner. The one brings his professional insights and understandings of the real-life situation he is handling; the other brings his reflective scientific objectivity, his tendency to formulate and generalize, and his more systematic procedures of exploration. Either without the other often arrives at misleading results. As the practitioner increasingly adopts a more exploratory and objective point of view toward his own professional practices, he will continue to develop new high standards of performance in his field as well as expedite the social science of social practice.

For Further Reading

For Further Reading

The literature in the field of intergroup relations numbers many hundreds of publications in the form of pamphlets, reports, and books. We think that the reader of this book may be interested, however, in a selected bibliography and particularly in those references which affected the authors' thinking and research activity. Consequently, from the vast mass of literature which the authors studied over a five-year period we have attempted to select for the reader those references which seem most useful and helpful to the practitioner. Obviously, such a list represents merely a beginning for the reader who desires to equip himself with a comprehensive knowledge of thinking and activity in the field of intergroup relations. The authors have added brief comments after each reference to give the reader some idea of its contents and relevance.

1. ALLPORT, GORDON W. *The Resolution of Intergroup Tensions.* New York: National Conference of Christians and Jews, 1951. Pamphlet.

    An evaluation of various methods to reduce intergroup tensions, based upon Allport's own research and a summary of the work of other social scientists. Especially helpful to teachers, field workers, and practitioners who feel the need for careful evaluation of the methods they use.

2. ALPENFELS, ETHEL J. *Sense and Nonsense about Race.* New York: Friendship Press, 1946. Pamphlet.

    Fallacies about differences in people are discussed helpfully and with humor in this pamphlet.

3. BARUCH, DOROTHY W. *Glass House of Prejudice.* New York: William Morrow & Co., 1946. Pp. 205.

    A psychologist discusses the causes and the results of prejudice against minority groups and concludes her study with suggested remedies.

4. BENEDICT, RUTH. *Race, Science, and Politics.* Rev. ed. New York: Viking Press, 1947. Pp. 206.

    A popular presentation which distinguishes between the actual anthropological facts and the arguments of racists.

5. BETTELHEIM, BRUNO. *Overcoming Prejudice.* Chicago: Science Research Associates, 1953. Pamphlet.

A prominent psychotherapist discusses the mental-health aspects of prejudice from the viewpoint of both the majority-group child and the minority-group child. He considers the causes of prejudice and analyzes the adult role in solving this problem.

6. BETTELHEIM, BRUNO, and LEWIN, KURT. *Securing Our Children against Prejudice.* New York: American Jewish Committee, 1952. Pamphlet.

Reprints of articles by two eminent social scientists presenting different positions on the most effective ways of making the children of minority and majority groups feel secure. A discussion guide is available.

7. *Democracy Demands It: A Resource Unit for Intercultural Education in the High School.* New York: Harper & Bros., 1950.

This publication presents as a resource unit many activities that teachers of science, social studies, and English will find helpful in eliminating racial prejudice.

8. DEUTSCH, MORTON, and COLLINS, MARY C. *Interracial Housing: A Psychological Evaluation of a Social Experiment.* Minneapolis: University of Minnesota Press, 1951. Pp. 173.

A study of comparable interracial projects in New York City and Newark, New Jersey. The report indicates that where housing was integrated, there was a reduction of prejudice and growth in harmonious intergroup relations.

9. FRAZIER, E. FRANKLIN. *The Negro in the United States.* New York: Macmillan Co., 1949. Pp. 767.

An up-to-date factual survey, extending from immigration from Africa to the current status of the American Negro. Written by an outstanding sociologist on the faculty of Howard University.

10. HEIGHT, DOROTHY I. *Step by Step with Interracial Groups.* Revised. New York: National Board of the Young Women's Christian Association, 1954. Pamphlet.

Discusses opportunities and problems arising in intergroup work in clubs and other groups. Takes up the needs of individuals, the role of the leader, education of parents, and questions of agency policy. This valuable pamphlet has been used to great advantage by many professionals working for youth-serving agencies.

11. HOGREFE, RUSSELL, SELLTIZ, CLAIRE, and COOK, STEWART. "Intergroup Relations in Leisure-Time Activities." New York:

Commission on Community Interrelations of the American Jewish Congress, 1954. Mimeographed.

A report on a research project that surveyed factors in the success and failure of various policies, programs, and staff attitudes in leisure-time agencies. A very insightful and valuable research document, deserving wide dissemination among practitioners.

12. *Interracial Practices in the YMCA: A Guide for Officers and Leaders of Local YMCAs.* Prepared by the National Study Commission on Intercultural Practices in the YMCA. New York: Association Press, 1953.

A guide designed by this youth-serving agency to achieve "a realistic harmony between its practices and its professed ideals." Discusses in detail the roles of boards and committees, the professional, and the membership in moving toward greater integration. Also indicates opportunities offered by program activities and some community relations problems.

13. *Inventory of Research in Racial and Cultural Relations,* Vol. V, Bull. 283 (winter, 1953). Chicago: Committee on Education, Training and Research in Race Relations of the University of Chicago, 1953.

This bulletin contains the proceedings of the Conference on Research Relations, held at the University of Chicago, July 26–30, 1952. The purpose of the conference was to assess the state of race relations research in the light of the practical needs for knowledge and the possibilities and resources for obtaining it. The conference was attended by a substantial portion of the people in the country who are doing significant research in the field. Particularly noteworthy among a series of excellent papers are the following: "Trends in Race Relations Research," by Herman H. Long, director, Race Relations Department, American Missionary Association, Fisk University; and "Evaluation of Research in Race Relations," by William C. Bradbury, of the University of Chicago.

14. LEIGHTON, ALEXANDER H. *The Governing of Men: General Principles and Recommendations Based on Experience at a Japanese Relocation Camp.* Princeton, N.J.: Princeton University Press, 1945. Pp. 404.

The author, a psychiatrist and social anthropologist, has drawn conclusions concerning the governing of men during times of stress based upon his observations at a relocation center for Japanese internees. His list of "principles" has aroused much favorable comment among community organizers and administrators.

15. LIPPITT, RONALD. *Training in Community Relations: A Research Exploration toward New Group Skills.* New York: Harper & Bros., 1949. Pp. 286.

Describes in detail training programs in intergroup relations, based on intensive research experiences. Valuable because it identifies some of the specific characteristics of effective leadership. Recommended reading for the experienced professional worker in community relations.

16. MacIVER, ROBERT M. *The More Perfect Union: A Program for the Control of Intergroup Discrimination in the United States.* New York: Macmillan Co., 1948. Pp. 311.

Recommendations for the attack upon discrimination on the economic, educational, and political fronts, written by a leading sociologist.

17. "Methods of Combating Discrimination: Descriptive Records Submitted to the World YWCA by the YWCA of the USA, 1954." Available from the National Board of the YWCA, 600 Lexington Avenue, New York, New York. Mimeographed.

A study and evaluation of the practices aiming at the integration of minority groups and the overcoming of religious, racial, social, and political prejudice.

18. MYRDAL, GUNNAR. *An American Dilemma.* New York: Harper & Bros., 1944. Pp. 1483.

One of the most comprehensive reports ever made on the Negro in American society.

19. *The Pen Is Mightier.* (A catalogue of publications in the field of community relations.) ("Community Relations Service Publications.") 386 Fourth Avenue, New York 16, New York: American Jewish Committee, 1954.

This catalogue is one of the most comprehensive published. The individual desiring to learn about books, pamphlets, and program aids for combating prejudice and eliminating discrimination may well start here. It contains excellent bibliographical references on civil and human rights; on discrimination in education, employment, fraternities, housing, and public accommodations; and on the relations among church, state, and educational institutions and combating prejudice.

20. POWDERMAKER, HORTENSE. *Probing Our Prejudices.* New York: Harper & Bros., 1944. Pp. 73.

We know that prejudices are not entirely due to lack of knowledge but that they lie also in the realm of the emotions. This small book is an attempt to help high-school students become aware of their prejudices, to understand the nature, origin, and effect of prejudices, and to suggest activities which can help reduce them. The book goes far in achieving its expressed aim.

21. SAENGER, GERHART. *The Social Psychology of Prejudice: Achieving Intercultural Understanding and Co-operation in a Democracy.* New York: Harper & Bros., 1953. Pp. 304.

Concerned with the contributions of the social sciences in dealing with the problems of prejudice and discrimination.

22. SAUNDERS, REDDING J. *On Being Negro in America.* Indianapolis: Bobbs-Merrill, 1951. Pp. 165.

Observations, based upon personal experience, on what it means to be a "second-class" citizen.

23. SIMPSON, GEORGE E., and YINGER, J. MILTON. *Racial and Cultural Minorities: An Analysis of Prejudice and Discrimination.* New York: Harper & Bros., 1953. Pp. 773.

A textbook dealing with the causes and consequences of prejudice and discrimination, with racial minorities in the social structure, and with the reduction of prejudice and discrimination. Has been found to be one of the most comprehensive college texts in race relations.

24. "Suggested Procedures for Developing Good Intercultural and Interracial Practices in Group Work and Recreation Agencies." Materials based on study by the Committee on Cultural Factors in Group Work of the American Service Institute, Margaret G. Owen, chairman. Pittsburgh, Pa.: American Service Institute. Mimeographed.

Very practical, immediate suggestions dealing with boards of directors, staff and membership roles, and participation in the intergroup relations aspect of the agency's program. The executive of a Y, Scout council, or neighborhood center will find this of great value in clarifying the "administrative" policy of the agency in intergroup relations.

25. THELEN, HERBERT A. *Dynamics of Groups at Work.* Chicago: University of Chicago Press, 1954.

Gathered from seven years of pioneering work by the Human Relations Laboratory of the University of Chicago. This excellent work describes and analyzes practice in the following six fields: citizen participation, classroom teaching, in-service professional training, administration and management, human relations training, and public meetings.

26. WATSON, GOODWIN, *Action for Unity.* Issued by the Commission on Community Interrelations of the American Jewish Congress. Pamphlet. A discussion guide based on this study is also available.

   An attempt to supply a strategic guide in the struggle against prejudice and persecution. An "exploratory survey" on how good will was put to work in the interest of better intergroup relations and an examination of the basic assumptions and approaches in this effort.

27. WILLIAMS, ROBIN M., JR. *The Reduction of Intergroup Tensions: A Survey of Research on Problems of Ethnic, Racial, and Religious Group-Relations.* (Bull. 57.) New York: Social Science Research Council, 1947. Pp. 153.

   "The author examines the more important techniques and procedures in use by representative action agencies. He analyzes the basic assumptions underlying the action programs and proposes research designed to test these assumptions" (quotation from Preface).

28. WITTENBERG, R. M. *So You Want To Help People.* New York: Association Press, 1947.

   One of the more popular, easy-to-read, yet scholarly, books on how to work with membership and staff in developing a professionally sound program, especially from the point of view of mental hygiene. The book contains insightful descriptions of the handling of race relations incidents.

29. WOLFE, ANN G. *Leaders' Guide: A Manual on Better Human Relations for Leaders in Youth Agencies.* New York: Division of Youth Service, American Jewish Committee, 1954. Pamphlet.

   Intended as a brief practical handbook for leaders of youth groups, this very valuable pamphlet discusses the goals of youth-serving agencies and the role of the group leader. It contains a helpful section on resources, listing pamphlets, films, and other program aids useful to the group leader.

30. WRIGHT, RICHARD. *Black Boy: A Record of Childhood and Youth.* New York: Harper & Bros., 1945. Pp. 228.

   A classic personal document in American literature. A sensitive young writer tells what it meant to grow up amid sordid surroundings in the South.

Acknowledgments

Acknowledgments

The authors are indebted to many friends and colleagues for their aid and counsel, particularly to the fruitful research collaboration with Robin M. Williams, Jr., and Edward A. Suchman, of Cornell University. Their advice and help has been invaluable.

Robert B. Johnson not only collaborated in the writing of chapters 1 and 2 but also aided the authors to gain deeper insight into the dynamics of human behavior in the minority community.

We are indebted to Mrs. Lois R. Dean, who served as a field worker and assisted in the analysis of the research data; to Mrs. Mildred Essick, who served as a field interviewer and also as secretary to one of the important human relations committees whose program and activities were studied intensively in the course of the research program.

The book was read in manuscript form by Miss Dorothy Height, of the YWCA, Miss Jean Maxwell, of the Graduate School of Public Administration and Social Service of New York University, and John McDowell, of the National Federation of Settlements. Their criticisms and suggestions helped us to adapt the material to the needs of the intergroup relations practitioner.

Mrs. Anna Lee Simon served as research assistant and was enormously helpful in the preparation of the manuscript.

The Cornell studies in intergroup relations, which are the source of many of the ideas presented in this book, were supported by the Rockefeller Foundation. A further research program to determine the specific application of these ideas to the practice of intergroup relations was made possible by a grant from Russell Sage Foundation. Grateful acknowledgment is made to each of these foundations for their encouragement and support.

While we have made much use of the advice and support of the individuals mentioned, responsibility for the statements and findings of the book rests with the authors.

PHOENIX BOOKS

PHOENIX BOOKS

PHOENIX BOOKS

 PHOENIX SCIENCE SERIES

PHOENIX BOOKS